It Takes a Certain Type to Be a Writer

And Hundreds of Other Facts from the World of Writing

Totally Riveting Utterly Entertaining Trivia

Erin Barrett and Jack Mingo

CONARI PRESS

First published in 2003 by Conari Press,
an imprint of Red Wheel/Weiser, LLC
York Beach, ME
With offices at:
368 Congress Street
Boston, MA 02210
www.redwheelweiser.com

Library of Congress Cataloging-in-Publication Data

Barrett, Erin.
  It takes a certain type to be a writer : and hundreds of other facts
from the world of writing / Erin Barrett and Jack Mingo.
      p. cm.—(Totally riveting utterly entertaining trivia)
Includes bibliographical references and index.
  ISBN 1-57324-722-7 (pbk.)
  1. Authorship—Miscellanea. 2. Authors—Anecdotes. I. Mingo,
Jack, 1952- II. Title. III. Series.
  PN165.B37 2003
  808'.02—dc21

                                                    2003002080

Typeset in Bulmer MT

Printed in Canada

TCP

10 09 08 07 06 05 04 03

 8 7 6 5 4 3 2 1

It Takes a Certain Type to Be a Writer

A Word from the Authors

A person who publishes a book willfully appears before the public with his pants down.
—Edna St. Vincent Millay

Who doesn't want to be a writer? Nearly all of us believe we've got a novel in us, or that we can write poems that will sing the body electric and make the angels cry.

What's interesting, though, is just how hard writing can be. Probably, for every hundred people who think they can write, only a small handful will give a good, disciplined try. For every hundred of those who start, only a few will finish their manuscripts. And for every hundred who do, only a few will get their work published. For every hundred who get published, only a few will make enough money to make a living. The writing life is difficult and full of frustration and neurosis. It takes a special type even to try it.

Writers who "make it" have to live with alternately being scorned and lionized by the people around them. They see the fruits of their labors going largely to the publishers and booksellers, who in return treat them as a necessary inconvenience. And anyone who writes has to wrestle with internal, if not external, editors and other demons every time she sits down to pen a phrase. If that isn't bad enough, if a writer's work sells, he knows that he may have to deal with seeing his baby, the one he brought to life with sweat and sacrifice, lacerated by bad reviews (or worse, neglected, with no reviews at all). What's surprising is that anybody would want to be a writer in the first place!

There must be something beyond rationality at work here. Call it love or obsession, a need to express or a need for attention, an ability to communicate or an inability to shut up, but writers are clearly a little bit insane. For example, poet Amy Lowell was so dependent on the joys of her Manila cigars that she bought 10,000 of them in 1915 for fear they'd be unavailable during wartime. Keats was known to have public fits of alternately laughing and weeping. And Percy Shelley and Lord

Byron both had delusions about being stalked by enemies.

Writers work like dogs, get almost no glory, and have to live with a pretty wacky reputation. If you're a writer, or want to be one, we salute you. And if you're the friend, relative, or lover of a writer, treat them gently and give them aid, comfort, and small loans. Buy them this book as encouragement. This book is meant to give heart to writers, both successful and aspiring, and to entertain anybody interested in the world of literature. We hope you'll enjoy it.

Erin Barrett
Jack Mingo

one

Don't Quit Your Day Job

"**I**n America you can make a fortune as a writer, but not a living."

—*James Michener*

Alas, this has always been the case. A few writers get rich; the rest eke out a living or are subsidized by inheritance or a patient spouse. Almost all writers have had to work another job to keep from starving.

A survey in 1978 by PEN, the international literary organization, was so depressing that the organization never bothered to update it. The survey found that the median annual income earned by published book writers was $4,700, with 68 percent making less than $10,000, and 9 percent earning nothing.

According to the latest from the U.S. Bureau of Labor and Statistics, beginning salaries for newspaper staff writers and editorial assistants top off at a whopping $21,000 annually—making them some of the lowest paying jobs of all. After five years on the job, they can expect to make about $30,000.

Senior editors at the largest newspapers average only about $67,000 as a top salary.

These are the salaried positions; a large proportion of writers and editors freelance, making their annual salaries even iffier, and job security nonexistent.

The most William Shakespeare earned for writing a play was £8 ($1,325 in today's money). He never made more than an annual income of £20 ($3,313) from his writing. Luckily, his acting career paid a lot better, and he owned some real estate, making him fairly prosperous.

Harriet Beecher Stowe got lucky. She was just a "poor professor's wife" when she wrote *Uncle Tom's Cabin.* Her book sold 3,000 copies on its day of publication, and within a year it had sold more than 300,000 copies in the United States alone.

"**T**o coin one's brain into silver is, to my thinking, the hardest job in the world."

—*Edgar Allan Poe*

Poe should know. It took him eighteen months of badgering to get paid after the *New York Mirror* published one of his poems. The poem was "The Raven," and the overdue payment was $10 ($178 in today's money).

"**W**ith the proceeds of my last novel, I purchased a small handbarrow, on which my guests' luggage is wheeled from the station to my house. It needs a coat of paint. With the proceeds of my next novel, I shall have it painted."

—*Henry James*

Before achieving his own fame, a young Sinclair Lewis sold plots and story ideas to Jack London.

Screenwriter Rod Serling was very reluctant to put himself in front of the camera to host his *Twilight Zone* TV show. In fact he had to routinely change shirts during filming because they became saturated with nervous sweat. His tense and terse delivery caught on, however, and he found himself spending more time on camera than writing. His creative output went further downhill a few seasons later when he was hired as host—without any creative input—for the abysmal *Night Gallery*. But at least he mercifully died during open-heart surgery before hitting rock bottom: he had been scheduled to begin hosting a 1976 comedy-variety show called *Keep on Truckin'*.

Dr. Pearl Zane Grey, a moderately successful dentist, became more successful by writing Western novels in between drilling patients (dropping the "Dr." and his first name for his literary works).

No wonder all of his stories were tinged with such paranoia: Franz Kafka was a civil servant who only dabbled with writing in his spare time.

Anthony Trollope worked for the British post office for thirty-three years. During that time he wrote four dozen novels by rising at 5:30 A.M. and writing a thousand words before trudging off to work. Within postal circles, however, his biggest claim to fame is that he invented the street-corner mailbox.

Another man of letters (literally!) was William Faulkner, who was postmaster of Oxford, Mississippi.

Charles Bukowski and Richard Wright both worked as mail carriers.

Leo Tolstoy found God and gave up writing fiction between 1878 and 1885 in favor of writing about his religious beliefs and society. He also gave up his property and sex life, denounced his former writings, and began working in the fields dressed as a peasant. Because of his fame as a former novelist, people made pilgrimages from all over the world to visit him and hear his word. The Russian Orthodox Church became so threatened by his ever-increasing spiritual power that, in 1901, it excommunicated him.

Horatio Alger wrote 134 rags-to-riches books about plucky poor boys being taken home and adopted by rich industrialists. His career as a Unitarian minister had been cut short in 1886 when a church committee investigated rumors of his "inordinate and imprudent" attention to the boys of his congregation. Accused of molesting two of them, he was allowed to resign his position. It was then that he began writing full time.

Erle Stanley Gardner, creator of Perry Mason, was himself a lawyer who rooted for the underdog. He was admitted to the California bar in 1911 and was known for defending poor Chinese and Mexican immigrants. In the 1940s, with some of his royalties, Gardner set up "The Court of Last Resort," an organization that took on cases of people who seemed unjustly imprisoned.

Poet Wallace Stevens was an executive in the legal department of the Hartford Insurance Company. An aside he was heard to mutter at one of his few poetry readings: "If only the boys back in the office could see me now."

Before they became the household names they are today, Cynthia Ozick, Dorothy Sayers, and Joseph Heller all wrote advertising copy.

Kurt Vonnegut wrote press releases for General Electric.

Amy Tan wrote horoscopes.

Before her literary career took off, Rita Mae Brown wrote screenplays, most notably for Roger Corman's schlock slasher film *Slumber Party Massacre* in 1982.

Henry David Thoreau was a pencil maker.

"O. Henry" (William Sydney Porter) began writing short stories while working as a bank teller. Unfortunately, he was convicted of embezzlement and was sentenced to five years in the federal penitentiary in Columbus, Ohio. His crime had attracted some notoriety, so he didn't want to use his real name for his writing. Porter tried out a number of pseudonyms before—true to his larcenous past—he "borrowed" the name of prison guard Orrin Henry.

Charles Dickens as a desperately poor child was forced to work at a shoe polish factory in London.

Young Langston Hughes was a busboy in a Washington, D.C., hotel, but it gave him an opportunity. At a formal dinner, he placed a packet of his poems next to poet Vachel Lindsay's plate. Lindsay liked what he saw and helped launch Hughes's career, making the former busboy a leading player in the Harlem Renaissance of the 1920s.

Henry Miller worked as a branch manager for Western Union for nearly five years, a period that he said was "comparable for me to Dostoyevksy's stay in Siberia."

In Abraham Lincoln's time, Walt Whitman labored as a low-level clerk in the U.S. Government's Indian Department (later called the Bureau of Indian Affairs). Whitman was a loyal employee—his mournful poem, "Oh Captain, My Captain," was written about Lincoln's assassination.

Another poet fared better in the federal bureaucracy. In 1905, E. A. Robinson had not sold a poem for five years when he got an out-of-the-blue fan letter from President Theodore Roosevelt. Roosevelt arranged to have his own publisher take Robinson on, talked favorably about his poetry from the "bully pulpit" of the presidency, and hired Robinson into the Customs Department in New York City. The poet's only responsibilities there were to open his roll-top desk, read the paper for a while, close his desk, and leave the paper on his chair as he left so that his boss would know he'd been there. When William Howard Taft took office, though, Robinson was unceremoniously informed that he'd have to actually start working. He quit immediately.

Henry Fielding, the author of *Tom Jones*, was London's first police magistrate.

In 1842, Washington Irving was appointed ambassador to Spain.

Julia Ward Howe should've gotten rich for writing the much-performed "Battle Hymn of the Republic" (even if she stole the melody from a song called "John Brown's

Body"). She didn't. In fact, Ward was paid a mere $4 from the *Atlantic Monthly*.

"In twenty years, I've never had a day when I didn't have to think about somebody else's needs. And this means the writing has to be fitted around it."

—*Alice Munro*

The first woman in history to actually earn a living as an author was probably Britisher Aphra Behn (1640–1689), who wrote a number of well-received plays, poems, and novels. She's buried in Westminster Abbey.

Other day jobs of famous writers:

- Honoré de Balzac: law clerk
- Daniel Defoe: seller of tobacco
- Oliver Wendell Holmes: physician
- Sir Arthur Conan Doyle: physician and ophthalmologist
- William Carlos Williams: pediatrician

- Benedict de Spinoza: lens grinder
- George Orwell: Indian Imperial Police Officer in Burma
- Paul Laurence Dunbar: elevator operator
- A. E. Houseman: clerk at the patent office
- Nathaniel Hawthorne: customs inspector
- Eric Hoffer: longshoreman
- Washington Irving: diplomat
- Herman Melville: sailor
- Charles Lamb: accountant
- Marianne Moore: librarian
- Vladimir Nabokov: entomologist
- Antoine de Saint-Exupéry: pilot
- Sir Walter Scott: attorney
- Lew Wallace: major general in the Union Army
- J. R. R. Tolkien: professor of Anglo-Saxon language and literature
- Thomas Hardy: architect

- Joseph Wambaugh: cop

- Tom Paine: corset maker

Profits & Loss

Mark Twain bought one of the first telephones in 1876, the same year that Alexander Graham Bell patented it. Unfortunately, though, his love of new inventions was his downfall. He invested the bulk of the fortune he had made from books—about $200,000, or the equivalent of almost $4 million in today's money—in an automatic typesetting machine that didn't pan out. As a result, he became unable to pay his debts in 1895 and had to embark on a series of new books and speaking tours to recoup at least some of his personal savings. His loss, our gain.

Jack London was the first American author to earn a million dollars from his writing.

He unfortunately lost the vast bulk of it to high living and bad investments.

Anaïs Nin wrote her famous erotica for hire because she needed the money. She had an anonymous rich patron who paid her $1 a page. She was told, "Take out all the poetry, it has to be nothing but descriptions of sex."

"I now have a library of nearly 900 volumes, over 700 of which I wrote myself."

—*Henry David Thoreau, putting the best possible face on a bad situation. His publisher had just sent him 706 unsold remainders (out of a thousand copies printed) of* A Week on the Concord & Merrimack Rivers.

Thomas Paine's revolutionary tract *Common Sense* sold 120,000 copies in the first three months of 1776. He could've made a fortune but ended up losing money on the deal. He had refused to take a penny of the profits, earmarking half for the publisher for taking the risk of being shut down by the British and the other half to buy mittens for Revolutionary Army troops. Unfortunately, the greedy publisher ended up taking it all. Worse, he had gotten Paine to pay the printer's bill and never reimbursed him for it.

Leo Tolstoy's library and manuscripts were destroyed by a mob of peasants in 1917.

Louisa May Alcott detested children but wrote *Little Women* solely because she was short of cash and her publisher demanded "a girl's story" from her.

Successful children's author Margaret Wise Brown went through her royalty checks as fast as she could get them. She blew her very first royalty check by purchasing a vendor's entire cart full of flowers.

two

If at First You Don't Succeed

There are hundreds of examples of publishers rejecting books that subsequently turned out to be bestsellers. Here are excerpts from actual rejection letters as collected in a wonderful book called *Rotten Rejections* by Andre Bernard:

- *The War of the Worlds* by H. G. Wells: "An endless nightmare. I do not believe it would take. . . . I think the verdict would be 'Oh don't read that horrid book.'"

- *The Bridge Over the River Kwai* by Pierre Boulle: "A very bad book."

- *The Good Earth* by Pearl S. Buck: "Regret that the American public is not interested in anything on China."

- *Sanctuary* by William Faulkner: "Good God, I can't publish this. We'd both be in jail."

- *Madame Bovary* by Gustave Flaubert: "You have buried your novel underneath a heap of details which are well done but utterly superfluous."

- *The Diary of Anne Frank* by Anne Frank: "The girl doesn't, it seems to me, have a special perception or feeling which would lift that book above the 'curiosity' level."

- *Lord of the Flies* by William Golding: "It does not seem to us that you have been wholly successful in working out an admittedly promising idea."

- *The Wind in the Willows* by Kenneth Grahame: "The form of the story is most unexpected."

- *The Last of the Plainsmen* by Zane Grey: "I do not see anything in this to convince me you can write either narrative or fiction."

- *Poem* by Sara Haardt: "This poem I can't take. We have 200 or 300 bales of poetry stored in Hoboken, in the old Norddeutscher-Lloyd pier. There are 300,000 poets in America."

- *Kon-Tiki* by Thor Heyerdahl: "The idea of men adrift on a raft does have a certain appeal, but for the most part this is a long, solemn and tedious Pacific voyage."

- *The Blessing Way* by Tony Hillerman: "If you insist on rewriting this stuff, get rid of all that Indian stuff."

- *A Portrait of the Artist as a Young Man* by James Joyce: "The point of view is not an attractive one."

- *The Naked and the Dead* by Norman Mailer: "Profanity and obscenity. . . . In my opinion it is barely publishable."

- *Lolita* by Vladimir Nabokov: "I am most disturbed at the thought that the writer has asked that this be published. I can see no possible cause that could be served by its publication. I recommend that it be buried under a stone for a thousand years."

- *Animal Farm* by George Orwell: "It is impossible to sell animal stories in the U.S.A."

- *Swann's Way (Remembrance of Things Past)* by Marcel Proust: "I can't see why a chap should need thirty pages to describe how he turns over in bed before going to sleep."

- *The Fountainhead* by Ayn Rand: "It is badly written and the hero is unsympathetic."

- *Cornhuskers* by Carl Sandburg: "Rather out of our line. I dare you to do us a soft and luscious lyric, capable of reducing a fat woman to sniffles."

- *And to Think That I Saw It on Mulberry Street* by Dr. Seuss: "It's too different from other juvenile books on the market to warrant its selling."

- *Lust for Life* by Irving Stone: "A long, dull novel about an artist."

- *A Confederacy of Dunces* by John Kennedy Toole: "Obsessively foul and grotesque."

- *The Time Machine* by H. G. Wells: "It is not interesting enough for the general reader and not thorough enough for the scientific reader."

- *Mankind in the Making* by H. G. Wells: "Only a minor writer of no large promise."

- *Leaves of Grass* by Walt Whitman: "We deem it injudicious to commit ourselves."

- *Lady Windermere's Fan* by Oscar Wilde: "My dear sir, I have read your manuscript. O, my dear sir."

three

What's in a Name?

O. SOGLOW

The Dewey Decimal System is named for Melvil Dewey, who developed it in 1876. Dewey served as the director of the New York State Library from 1889 to 1906 and founded the American Library Association in 1876. He also started the first library school in America in 1887, at Columbia University.

You've likely heard of the *Scarlet Pimpernel,* but perhaps you've wondered—what exactly is a pimpernel? No, not a type of dark bread nor a backup singer for Gladys Knight . . . a pimpernel is a type of primrose that also comes in blue, purple, and white and was once known as "the poor man's weather glass" because its flowers close at the approach of bad weather. Author Emmuska Orczy, an English baroness born in Hungary, had her character in the story use a pimpernel as his flower calling card, the way the Lone Ranger used a silver bullet and Zorro used a *Z.*

The Postman Always Rings Twice had nothing to do with the mail service. The title was a private joke of author James Cain. His postman would ring his doorbell twice whenever the many-times-rejected book's manuscript came back from a publisher.

You might well wonder where Sir A. Conan Doyle came up with the name "Sherlock Holmes." The detective began as "Sherrinford Hope," which clearly wasn't up to snuff, so the cricket-playing author adopted the last name of a player named Mordecai Sherlock on a rival Cricket team from Yorkshire. The "Hope" had come from the whaling ship *Hope,* but Doyle replaced it in honor of Oliver Wendell Holmes who, like Doyle, happened to be a writer/doctor.

Sam Spade's first name was a secondhand discard—mystery writer Samuel Dashiell Hammett had stopped using his first name years earlier.

Have you read the bestseller *Tomorrow Is Another Day?* No? It's about a southern belle named Pansy, and was written by Atlanta newspaper writer Peggy Marsh. Still don't recognize it? True, the name of the book, the main character, and even the author got changed a bit in the editing process. For example, Pansy became "Scarlet O'Hara." You can probably figure out the rest.

An even more extreme transformation happened in the writing of the novel *Harvey,* the story about the 6-foot-1-inch rabbit that could be seen only by one Elwood P. Dowd. In the first draft, author Mary Chase called the character "Daisy." Daisy was only 4 feet tall, and she was a canary.

Mystery writer "Ellery Queen" was really two people: ad copywriter Frederic Dannay, and his cousin, publicity agent Manfred Lee (originally Lepovski). They decided to write their stories in the first person, as if written by their detective named Ellery Queen, so to keep the illusion going, they gave him the author's credit.

The poet who called himself by the lower-cased "e. e. cummings" did have a real name behind the initials: Edward Estlin Cummings. With capital letters, even.

"Rebecca West" was the name of a character in a play by Henrik Ibsen. When Cicily Isabel Fairfield needed a pen name, she took the name of the character, which was a role she'd played in a school production.

Andrew Barton Patterson appears on the Australian $10 note. Patterson was the author of such Australian classics as *The Man from Snowy River*. However, in Australia the man is better known as "Banjo" Patterson, the jolly swagman who wrote all those billabong and jumbuck words to "Waltzing Matilda."

Dissatisfied with his given name, the writer of *Oz,* L. Frank Baum, eventually just dropped "Lyman" as his first name. Before that, he had also tried out writing children's stories under the pseudonyms Floyd Akers, Schuyler Stanton, and Edith Van Dyne.

Tennessee Williams wasn't really named Tennessee. In fact, he wasn't even from Tennessee. He was born Tom Williams from Mississippi, but somehow got the nickname "Tennessee" while living in New York City.

"Edna St. Vincent Millay" has a classy sound to it, doesn't it? Well, the real story isn't quite as upper crust as the name. Doctors at St. Vincent's Hospital in New York saved the life of Edna's uncle, so her mother honored the hospital by adding it to her unborn baby's name.

Maya Angelou's given name was Marguerite Johnson. "Maya Angelou" was a stage name she adopted as an exotic dancer at the Purple Onion, a Beat-era cabaret in San Francisco.

Kid author Margaret Wise Brown kept six publishers busy with her prolific output. To keep from flooding the market, she adopted pen names, including Golden MacDonald, Juniper Sage, Kaintuck Brown, and Timothy Hay.

Charles Dickens was born Charles Barrow, but for his literature went by his mother's maiden name. Before that, he wrote under the pseudonym "Boz."

Ernest Hall decided he liked his mother's given name better, so became Ernest Hemingway. Ditto George Bernard Carr, who went with his mom's "Shaw."

Joseph Conrad was born "Jòsef Korzeniowski" in Poland. The remarkable writer didn't even learn English until he was seventeen.

Veterinarian Alfred Wight decided that James Herriot would make a bright and beautiful pen name. He was right.

"Saki" was the pen name of Hecto Hugh Munro, who wrote wonderful short stories before he died in World War I. He took the name, not from Japanese rice wine (spelled *sake),* but from a wine-serving wench in a poem, "The Rubaiyat of Omar Khayyam." Probably reflecting an ancestor's profession, Persian poet Omar Khayyam's last name means "tent maker."

The *F* in F. Scott Fitzgerald stood for "Francis." He was named after a second cousin thrice removed who was named Francis Scott Key. Yes, *that* Francis Scott Key, the lawyer and amateur poet who wrote the words that became the United States' national anthem.

Pearl S. Buck is the only woman writer to have won both the Pulitzer Prize and the Nobel Prize in Literature. The "Buck" came from the name of her first husband; the *S* stood for "Sydenstricker," her birth name.

"**M**ark Twain" is a riverboat term meaning "two fathoms" (a depth of 12 feet). Samuel Clemens admitted that he wasn't the first author to use the pen name. A noted steamboat captain named Isaiah Sellers had used the pen name "Mark Twain" in essays and letters to New Orleans and St. Louis newspapers, and Clemens borrowed the name when he began parodying the distinguished river pilot's newspaper letters.

Ever wonder about the pet names of famous lovers? Gertrude Stein and Alice B. Toklas mostly called one another "Pussy" and "Lovey." But Gertrude's other pet names for Alice included "Cake" and "Lobster," while Alice called Gertrude "Mount Fattie" and "Fattuski."

Booker T. Washington was freed as a young child from slavery and was sent to school for the first time. Known all his life only as "Booker," it was then that he realized that the other kids had first and last names. Worried about being embarrassed, he decided as he entered the classroom to adopt a distinguished name from history as his own.

Later in life, Washington discovered that his mother had given him the last name

"Taliaferro" when he was born but had neglected to tell anybody, so Booker Washington added *T* as his middle initial.

It's usually just called *Moll Flanders,* but that's not the real title of Daniel Defoe's book. It's really *The Fortunes & Misfortunes of the Famous Moll Flanders Who was Born in Newgate, and during a Life of continu'd Variety for Threescore Years, besides her Childhood, was Twelve Year a Whore, five times a Wife (whereof once to her own Brother), Twelve Year a Thief, Eight Year a Transported Felon in Virginia, at last grew Rich, liv'd Honest, and dies a Penitent. Written from her own Memorandums* . . .

Have you ever read *First Impressions,* a three-volume novel by Anonymous? Don't be too sure you haven't. After the first printing in 1813, the book was rereleased as *Pride and Prejudice,* and its author, Jane Austen, decided to take credit for it.

Lesser-known works by George Bernard Shaw include the unlikely titles of *The Intelligent Woman's Guide to Socialism and Capitalism* and *The Adventures of the Black Girl in Her Search for God.*

Sometimes an author is fated to write a specific book. This is a list of reportedly genuine book titles and their authors:

- *A Treatise on Madness* by William Battie, M.D. (1768)

- *Riches and Poverty* by L. G. Chiozza Money (1905)

- *The Boy's Own Aquarium* by Frank Fin (1922)

- *How to Live a Hundred Years or More* by George Fasting (1927)

- *Diseases of the Nervous System* by Walter Russell Brain (1933)

- *Causes of Crime,* by A. Fink (1938)

- *Your Teeth* by John Chipping (1967)

- *The Cypress Garden* by Jane Arbor (1969)

- *Running Duck* by Paula Gosling (1979)

- *Motorcycling for Beginners* by Geoff Carless (1980)

- *Writing with Power* by Peter Elbow (1981)

- *Crocheting Novelty Potholders* by L. Macho (1982)

- *Illustrated History of Gymnastics* by John Goodbody (1983)

four

The Ties That Bind . . . and Sometimes Gag

whitney Darrow Jr.

"**W**riters write for fame, wealth, power, and the love of women."

—*Sigmund Freud*

It was because his wife Susan called his bluff and bluster that James Fenimore Cooper began writing novels. James was reading a new English novel out loud and after a few chapters tossed it aside. "I could write you a better book than that myself." Retorted Susan: "That's absurd, you don't even like writing letters." His honor injured, James began writing immediately.

Peter Benchley, author of *Jaws,* was just following the family business. His father was children's author Nathaniel Benchley; his grandfather, humorist Robert Benchley.

According to prevalent speculation, Kay Thompson modeled her Eloise character, the neglected rich girl who lived in a penthouse, after a young Liza Minnelli. What's the evidence? Thompson was Liza's godmother; Liza was about the same age as Eloise when Thompson wrote the first book; and recordings of Thompson performing Eloise sound a lot like the adult Minnelli.

In the breakup of the love affair between the poet Alfred de Musset and George Sand, one of the things that threatened Musset professionally and personally was awakening after a night of passion and finding Sand already awake and scratching away at her manuscripts by moonlight.

After Sand left Musset for another man, Musset took revenge by writing *Gamiani,* a pornographic novel about her.

Norman Mailer once stabbed his wife and then wrote a novel about it *(An American Dream).*

There was something a wee bit strange about Oscar Wilde. In retrospect, we suspect that his first fiancée, Florence Balcom, was relieved that she decided to marry author Bram Stoker instead.

In 1928, Evelyn Waugh, British writer of morals and manners between the two World Wars, married a woman who also was named Evelyn . . . Evelyn Gardner, the daughter of a lord. To avoid confusion, their friends called them "He-Evelyn Waugh" and "She-Evelyn Waugh." Mercifully (for everyone but He-Evelyn), the problem was solved a year later when She-Evelyn ran off with their friend, John Heygate.

Brokenhearted He-Evelyn quickly got the last word, though, and we do mean that literally—he depicted his ex-wife as the shrewish, adulterous "Lady Brenda Last" in his novel *A Handful of Dust*.

Oscar Wilde, though married with children, was very openly homosexual. Walt Whitman also was self-assuredly gay. When the two men met, the much older Whitman scandalized onlookers by kissing Wilde square on the lips.

Few people realize that children's author Roald Dahl was married to actress Patricia Neal. This was in 1953, after her scandalous affair with Gary Cooper. He helped her through a series of debilitating strokes in the 1960s. They divorced in 1983 after nearly thirty years of marriage, and he quickly remarried.

The character of Dill in Harper Lee's *To Kill a Mockingbird* was based on Truman Capote. Lee and Capote had been childhood friends in Monroeville, Alabama, at the time of the Scottsboro Boys trial. Later, as adults, Lee joined Capote in Kansas as he did research for *In Cold Blood*.

Edgar Allan Poe married his thirteen-year-old cousin.

Of the members of the famous Algonquin Round Table who traded quips and barbs at the Algonquin Hotel in New York City, almost all of them were writers like Dorothy Parker and Robert Benchley. One notable exception was Harpo Marx.

You'd imagine from his onscreen persona that Harpo would be tongue-tied among a group of writers, but he gave as good as he got. He had a number of literary friendships, including a close one with George Bernard Shaw.

When he first met George Bernard Shaw, Harpo was wrapped in a towel, having just emerged from a nude swim. Shaw reached out as if to shake Harpo's hand, but at the last minute jerked his towel away leaving him naked. "And this," the seventy-four-year-old playwright said, a twinkle in his eye, "is Mrs. Shaw," gesturing to the dignified lady standing nearby. Harpo and the Shaws quickly became fast friends.

Writers Named William

William Saroyan was a serious playwright. What most literature lovers don't know, though, is that he and his cousin also once cowrote a novelty song that was made into a hit by Rosemary Clooney. The song was "Come on a My House," and his cousin was Ross Bagdasarian, who later became famous as "David Seville" in creating the singing Chipmunks ("Alvin and His Harmonica," among others).

William wasn't Mrs. Shakespeare's only little boy. He had three brothers: Gilbert, Richard, and Edmund.

William S. Burroughs was the grandson of a man with the same name who invented the adding machine.

Despite being a self-avowed junkie and homosexual, Burroughs was a real lady-killer. We mean literally. One long night in Mexico filled with drinking and drugs, he tried to shoot a martini glass off the head of his common-law wife Joan with a pistol. He missed, hitting her in the forehead, killing her. Charged with involuntary manslaughter, he fled Mexico.

"I am forced to the appalling conclusion that I would never have become a writer but for Joan's death, and to a realization of the extent to which this event has motivated and formulated my writing," wrote

Burroughs three decades later. "The death of Joan brought me in contact with the invader, the Ugly Spirit and maneuvered me into a lifelong struggle, in which I have had no choice except to write my way out."

Coincidental Connections

Separated at birth? Diarist Anaïs Nin and surreal novelist Raymond Queneau both were born in France on February 21, 1903.

If you want to be poet laureate of the United States, it might help if you were born on March 1. Three of the nine poet laureates were born on that date—Howard Nemerov, Richard Wilbur, and Robert Hass.

Novelist Ernest Hemingway and poet Hart Crane were both born on July 21, 1899. Both had problems with alcoholism and depression, and both died by their own hands.

Authors Miguel de Cervantes and William Shakespeare both died on the same day—April 23, 1616.

Authors Kurt Vonnegut and Dr. Suess (Ted Geisel) were frat brothers in college.

Poets William Cullen Bryant and Henry Wadsworth Longfellow were both descendents of *Mayflower* settlers John and Priscilla Alden. Longfellow wrote about the couple in his fictional poem, "The Courtship of Miles Standish."

What do Ernest Hemingway, Dashiell Hammett, e. e. cummings, W. Somerset Maugham, John Dos Passos, Archibald

MacLeish, and Walt Disney have in common? They all drove ambulances during World War I.

Death of a Loved One

Writers often have deep love/hate relationships with the characters they write. E. B. White was so affected by the death of his fictional web spinner Charlotte that when he recorded the book on tape, it took nineteen takes before he could read it without his voice cracking.

When Charles Dickens allowed Little Nell to die in *The Old Curiosity Shop,* he wrote to a friend, "I am the wretchedest of the wretched. It casts the most horrible shadow upon me, and it is as much as I can do to keep moving at all. . . . Nobody will miss her like I shall."

Wrote Harriet Beecher Stowe about the death of her character, Eva: "It was like a death in my own family, and it affected me so deeply that I could not write a word for two weeks afterward."

On the other hand, Sir A. Conan Doyle grew to detest his detective Sherlock Holmes and killed him off with satisfaction. The rest of the world didn't agree: London stockbrokers wore armbands, the public deluged newspapers with letters of mourning and outrage, and a woman even picketed Doyle's house with a sign calling him a murderer.

five

Tips & Tricks
of the Trade

Charles Dickens always slept facing north. He also faced north when he wrote. At the time, many people believed that magnetic currents could affect bodily energies and that facing magnetic north would give beneficial results.

Virginia Woolf wrote standing up at an artist's desk.

Edmond Rostand, author of *Cyrano de Bergerac,* liked to write in the bathtub.

Raymond Carver wrote in his car. So did Gertrude Stein, who had a particular affinity for Fords.

Marcel Proust wrote in bed, swaddled in blankets, gloves, and scarves, in a room that he'd had lined with cork.

Perhaps this is why he was so prolific: Voltaire drank seventy cups of coffee a day.

Samuel Taylor Coleridge wrote *Kubla Khan* while high on opium. Perhaps drugs are not the answer to writers' block: The poem ends abruptly with an anticlimactic thud via the poet's notation that he can't finish because somebody knocked on his door.

"It's not a bad idea to get in the habit of writing down one's thoughts. It saves one from having to bother anyone else with them."

—*Isabel Colegate*

Before the days of word processing, how did authors keep track of their various drafts and revisions? Purple prose writer Jacqueline Susann typed each draft on different colors of paper: yellow for the first draft, then blue, pink, and finally white.

Ernest Hemingway would use only No. 2 pencils for his first drafts.

How do you prepare to write? Willa Cather read a passage from the Bible before sitting down to write.

It's a good rule of thumb to have outside interests while you write. For instance, in his spare time, John Dos Passos invented the Soap Bubble Gun.

Mark Twain loved gadgets, and would buy the latest thing when it came out. When typewriters hit the market, he was among the first to buy one (which he called "a curiosity-breeding little joker") for the then-outrageous price of $125 (more than $2,150 in today's money).

Twain was also the first author ever to submit a typewritten manuscript to a publisher. It was in 1883, and the book was *Life on the Mississippi*.

Twain used the "hunt and peck" typing method. He didn't know the touch-typing system of using all the fingers. Nobody did, because it wouldn't be invented for another quarter-century.

Twain eventually traded his Remington typewriter for a $12 saddle.

Oxford scholar J. R. R. Tolkien didn't care much for the modern world. Among other things, he never owned a car.

Tolkien was also a procrastinating perfectionist, which explains why it took him fourteen years to write his 1,000-page masterpiece, *The Lord of the Rings*. The book ran about a half million words, which sounds impressive, but if measured over fourteen years, that averages out to an output of fewer than a hundred words a day.

Poet E. A. Robinson was having dinner with an enthusiastic young novelist who announced that she never wrote any fewer than 5,000 words a day. Robinson responded, "This morning I deleted the hyphen from 'hell-hound' and made it one word; this afternoon I redivided it and restored the hyphen."

Not a bad idea: Novelist Frank Norris liked to recruit friends to point at him in restaurants and stage-whisper excitedly, "That's him!"

When asked what one book he would want if marooned on a desert island, essayist G. K. Chesterton eschewed the Bible, the collected works of Shakespeare, and the other usual responses to the question. "I would choose *Thomas's Guide to Practical Shipbuilding*," he said.

six

Everyone's a Critic

"A bad review is like baking a cake with all the best ingredients and having someone sit on it."

—*Danielle Steele*

"'Alice's Adventures in Wonderland'—We fancy that any real child might be more puzzled than enchanted by this stiff, over-wrought story."

—*Reviewers in* Children's Books *(1865)*

"The author should be kicked out from all decent society as below the level of the brute. He must be some escaped lunatic raving in pitiable delirium."

—*Review by the* Boston Intelligencer *of Walt Whitman's* Leaves of Grass *(1855)*

During his lifetime, Herman Melville was most famous for *Typee: A Peep at Polynesian Life,* his account of having lived after a shipwreck that left him a captive of Polynesian cannibals. His later novels, including *Moby Dick* and *Billy Budd*, were universally dismissed as dull, poorly written, incoherent, and full of metaphysical claptrap.

"Pay no attention to what the critics say: there has never been set up a statue in honor of a critic."

—*Jean Sibelius*

"The public is the only critic whose opinion is worth anything at all."

—*Mark Twain*

"If all grammarians in the world were placed end to end, it would be a good thing."

—*Oscar Wilde*

"I am forced to say that I have many fiercer critics than myself."

—*Irwin Shaw*

"**A**s a work of art, it has the same status as a long conversation between two not very bright drunks."

—*Clive James, reviewing Judith Krantz's*
Princess Daisy

"**F**rom the moment I picked up your book until I laid it down, I was convulsed with laughter. Some day I intend to read it."

—*Groucho Marx's blurb for S. J. Perelman's*
Dawn Ginsberg's Revenge

"**T**he only people who like to write terribly are those that do."

—*Franklin Pierce Adams*

When D. H. Lawrence showed his first novel to his coal miner father, his father asked "Davy, what dun they gie thee for that, lad?" "Fifty pounds, father," said young David Herbert. "Fifty pounds! And tha's niver done a day's hard work in thy life!"

"Why don't you write books that people can read?"

—*Nora Joyce, to her husband James*

Louisa May Alcott wasn't much of a free-speech advocate when it came to rival children's authors. She was on the committee that banned Huck Finn as "trash suitable only for the slums" from the Concord Library in Massachusetts. "If Mr. Clemens cannot think of something better to tell our pure-minded lads and lasses," she added, "he had best stop writing for them."

Mae West wasn't just a campy actress, but a playwright as well. Her first play, *Sex,* written in 1926, was about a Canadian prostitute. A production in New York City led to her imprisonment for more than a week on obscenity charges. Her second play, *Drag,* was about transvestites. It got shut down on Broadway before it could even open.

Fightin' Words

"**H**enry James writes fiction as if it were a painful duty."

—*Oscar Wilde*

"**I**n two-thirds of a page, James Fenimore Cooper has scored 114 offenses against literary art out of a possible 115. It breaks the record."

—*Mark Twain*

"**E**dgar Allan Poe was an unmanly sort of man whose love life seems to have been largely confined to crying in laps and playing mouse."

—*W. H. Auden*

"**G**eorge Bernard Shaw writes plays for the ages—the ages between five and twelve."

—*George Nathan*

"**V**irginia Woolf's writing is no more than glamorous knitting. I believe she must have a pattern somewhere."

—Dame Edith Sitwell

"**D**ame Edith Sitwell is a poisonous thing of a woman, lying, concealing, flipping, plagiarizing, misquoting, and being as clever a crooked literary publicist as ever."

—Dylan Thomas

"**G**ertrude Stein was a master at making nothing happen very slowly."

—Clifton Fadiman

"**M**ark Twain was a hack writer who would have been considered fourth rate in Europe, who tried out a few of the old proven 'sure-fire' literary skeletons with sufficient local color to intrigue the superficial and the lazy."

—William Faulkner

"In conversation Noah Webster is even duller than in writing, if that is possible."

—*Juliana Smith*

"Louisa May Alcott preserves to the age of fifty-six that contempt for ideas which is normal among boys and girls of fifteen."

—*Odell Shepherd*

"Lord Byron is mad, bad and dangerous to know."

—*Lady Caroline Lamb*

"I could readily see in Ralph Waldo Emerson, not withstanding his merit, a gaping flaw. It was the insinuation that had he lived in those days when the world was made, he might have offered some valuable suggestions."

—*Herman Melville*

"None of these people have anything to say, and none of them can write. It isn't writing at all—it's typing."

—*Truman Capote, about the Beat novelists*

"Of Dickens' style it is impossible to speak in praise. It is jerky, ungrammatical, and created by himself in defiance of rules. . . . No young novelist should ever dare to imitate the style of Dickens."

—*Anthony Trollope*

"There are two ways of disliking poetry; one way is to dislike it, the other is to read Alexander Pope."

—*Oscar Wilde*

"The ineffable dunce Oscar Wilde has nothing to say and says it with a liberal embellishment of bad delivery, embroidering it with reasonless vulgarities of attitude, gesture and attire. There never was an impostor so hateful, a blockhead so stupid, a crank so variously and offensively daft. He makes me tired."

—Ambrose Bierce

"**O**scar Wilde's talent seems to me to be essentially rootless, something growing in glass on a little water."

—George Moore

"**J**ohn Dryden's imagination resembles the wings of an ostrich."

—Thomas Babington Macaulay

"**L**ike most poets, preachers and metaphysicians, Ralph Waldo Emerson bursts into conclusions at a spark of evidence."

—Henry Seidel Canby

"**E**rnest Hemingway has never been known to use a word that might send a reader to the dictionary."

—William Faulkner

"**P**oor Faulkner. Does he really think big emotions come from big words?"

—*Ernest Hemingway*

"**H**enry James had a mind so fine that no idea could violate it."

—*T. S. Eliot*

"**I**f it were thought that anything I wrote was influenced by Robert Frost, I would take that particular piece of mine, shred it, and flush it down the toilet, hoping not to clog the pipes."

—*James Dickey*

Not all writers rushed to Salman Rushdie's defense in 1989 when his *Satanic Verses* stirred up death threats and *jihads* from conservative Muslims. In interviews and a letter to the *London Times*, children's author Roald Dahl accused Rushdie of being a "dangerous opportunist" and a "twit" who "clearly has profound knowledge of the Muslim religion and its people and he must have been totally aware of the deep and violent feelings his book would stir up among devout Muslims." He accused Rushdie of deliberately creating a sensation to get his "indifferent" book onto bestseller lists: "To my mind it is a cheap way of doing it."

Bard Reviews

Diarist Samuel Pepys (1633–1703) saw the original Shakespearean production of *A Midsummer Night's Dream* and called it "the most insipid, ridiculous play that I ever saw in my life."

Voltaire called Shakespeare's work a "vast dunghill" and wrote, "Shakespeare is a drunken savage with some imagination whose plays please only in London and Canada." Comparing him to Pierre Corneille, the great French playwright Voltaire also wrote, "Shakespeare is the Corneille of London, but everywhere else he is thought a great fool...."

"*Hamlet* is a vulgar and barbarous drama, which would not be tolerated by the vilest populace of France, or Italy.... One would imagine this piece to be the work of a drunken savage."

—*Voltaire*

"I have tried lately to read Shakespeare, and found it so intolerably dull that it nauseated me."

—*Charles Dickens*

"With the single exception of Homer, there is no eminent writer, not even Sir Walter Scott, whom I can despise so entirely as I despise Shakespeare when I measure my mind against his. The intensity of my impatience with him occasionally reaches such a pitch, that it would positively be a relief to me to dig him up and throw stones at him."

—*George Bernard Shaw*

"**S**hakespeare never has six lines together without a fault. Perhaps you may find seven, but this does not refute my general assertion."

—*Samuel Johnson*

"**S**hakespeare's name, you may depend on it, stands absurdly too high and will go down. He has no invention as to stories, none whatever. He took all his plots from old novels, and threw their stories into a dramatic shape, at as little expense of

thought as you or I could turn his plays
back again into prose tales."

—Lord Byron

"Shakespeare's stories are rude, immoral,
vulgar and senseless."

—Leo Tolstoy

"Now we sit through Shakespeare in order
to recognize the quotations."

—Oscar Wilde

"Never did any author precipitate himself
from such heights of thought to so low ex-
pressions, as Shakespeare often does. He is
the very Janus of poets; he wears, almost
everywhere, two faces: and you have scarce
begun to admire the one, e'er you despise
the other."

—John Dryden

Self-Criticism

"**I**f I could do this book [*The Grapes of Wrath*] properly, it would be one of the really fine books. But I am assailed by my own ignorance and inability."

—*John Steinbeck*

"**I**t took me fifteen years to discover that I had no talent for writing, but I couldn't give it up because by that time I was too famous."

—*Robert Benchley*

"**O**ne should never criticize one's own work except in a fresh and hopeful mood. The self-criticism of a tired mind is suicide."

—*Charles Norton Cooley*

"**I** scarcely look with full satisfaction upon any of my books, for they do not seem what they might have been. I often wish that I could have twenty years more, to take them down from the shelf one by one, and write them over."

—*Washington Irving*

seven

Stranger Than Fiction

"Truth is stranger than fiction, but it is because fiction is obliged to stick to possibilities. Truth isn't."

—*Mark Twain*

What's the matter with kids, anyway? Thomas Chatterton was a brilliant young English poet of the eighteenth century who at age seventeen wrote a successful burlesque opera, *The Revenge*. That same year, he convinced the literary world that, while poking around a church in Bristol, he had found a 300-year-old stack of inventively romantic and emotional poems written by a monk named Thomas Rowley. The "Rowley" poems—actually penned by Chatterton himself in faux Middle English— became wildly popular. However, in 1770, facing exposure as a fraud and unable to sell his own poetry, the eighteen-year-old poet killed himself. Regardless, his "Rowley" poems continued to be popular and greatly influenced the works of England's Romantic poets.

Most historians now believe that Aesop—the slave who allegedly authored fables in the sixth century B.C.—was about as real as Uncle Remus. In other words, he probably never existed.

Most of the fables attributed to Aesop were actually written in the first century A.D. by the Greek writer Valerius Babrius, who combined oral traditional fables with stories from India, and were translated into Latin by the Roman poet Phaedrus in the second century.

Agatha Christie nearly pulled off a real-life hoax worthy of her mystery novels. Upset that her husband was leaving her for another woman, she set up an incriminating scene that almost got him arrested for her "murder." Luckily for him, an employee at a distant seaside hotel saw news photos of Christie and recognized her as the woman who had slipped into the hotel under an assumed name. Although Christie claimed amnesia, the police were not amused after having wasted a week of searching rivers and bogs.

Poet Ezra Pound wrote *The Pisan Cantos* while imprisoned at a U.S. Army camp in Pisa, Italy. He had been arrested for treason because he had broadcast Fascist propaganda from Italy during World War II. Eventually judged insane, Pound spent twelve years in a Washington, D.C., mental hospital before returning to Italy.

How many books did Adolf Hitler write? Just the one, *Mein Kampf.* But that didn't mean that the editors of *Stern* magazine in Germany couldn't let their hopes get in the way of their good sense. In 1983, they bought the rights to publish twenty-six volumes of "Hitler's diaries" for a whopping $3.8 million. The hoax was good enough to fool the magazine's historian consultants. The plot finally unraveled when writing experts determined that the handwriting was not quite right. Furthermore, a fiber analysis uncovered that the books' binding contained polyester . . . a fabric that didn't come into use until the 1950s. Konrad Kujau, the perpetrator of the hoax, had practiced copying Hitler's handwriting for two years. He was sentenced to three years in jail.

Author Clifford Irving was sentenced to two and a half years in jail for misrepresenting an "autobiography" of Howard Hughes that Irving himself had written. The author had counted on the likelihood that the reclusive billionaire would not emerge from his penthouse bunker to publicly disavow the book . . . but he guessed wrong.

Another hoax is still accepted by many as genuine. *The Education of Little Tree* by Forrest Carter was purported to be the genuine memoir of a Cherokee orphan learning the ways of his tribe and nature while struggling to live in a white world. The book, still in print, turns out to have been written by a white supremacist and Ku Klux Klan member named *Asa* Carter.

Asa Carter's other claim to infame: As a writer for Alabama governor George Wallace, he penned the speech in which the governor vowed, "Segregation now! Segregation tomorrow! Segregation forever!" in response to federal pressure to integrate Alabama's public schools.

Alice B. Toklas was unjustly credited with inventing those famous hashish brownies. Actually, she may have been the victim of a hoax. When, in 1954, seventy-seven-year-old Toklas decided to publish her best recipes, she augmented the book by asking friends for their favorites. Hipster filmmaker Bryon Gysin was also a pot-smoking prankster, and he contributed a recipe for "Haschich Fudge," which he described as "the food of paradise. . . . It might provide an entertaining refreshment for a Ladies' Bridge Club or a chapter meeting of the D.A.R. . . . Euphoria and brilliant storms of laughter; ecstatic reveries and extensions of one's personality on several simultaneous planes are to be complacently expected. . . . It should be eaten with care. Two pieces are quite sufficient." Toklas either didn't get the joke or perhaps was delighted by it. Either way, the recipe appeared in the first edition of her cookbook but then was yanked from subsequent editions by the publisher.

eight

Quoth the Writer

"It takes the publishing industry so long to produce books, it's no wonder so many are posthumous."

—*Teressa Skelton*

"A person who publishes a book appears willfully in public with his pants down."

—*Edna St. Vincent Millay*

"Every author is a son of a bitch."

—*Horace Liveright*

"Writers aren't exactly people, they're a whole lot of people trying to be one person."

—*F. Scott Fitzgerald*

"I don't believe the good people of Mississippi ever will understand how a man can sit in the shade and make $30,000 for defacing a few scraps of paper. In Mississippi the people work for their money and you

can understand how they feel about writing, why it puzzles them."

—*William Faulkner, anticipating the reaction
of the home folks after he won the Nobel Prize
in 1961*

"In reality, people read because they want to
write. Anyway, reading is a sort of rewriting."

—*Jean-Paul Sartre*

"No government has ever loved great writers, only minor ones."

—*Aleksandr Solzhenitsyn*

"The multitude of books is a great evil.
There is no limit to this fever for writing."

—*Martin Luther*

"I no more thought of style or literary excellence than the mother who rushes into
the street for help to save her children from

a burning house thinks of the teachings of the rhetorician or the elocutionist."

—*Harriet Beecher Stowe*

"**N**othing stinks like a pile of unpublished writing."

—*Sylvia Plath*

"**O**utside of a dog, a book is man's best friend. Inside of a dog, it's too dark to read."

—*Groucho Marx*

"**W**hen I was a young boy, they called me a liar. Now that I'm grown up, they call me a writer."

—*Isaac Bashevis Singer*

"**W**riting is like prostitution. First you do it for the love of it, then you do it for a few friends, and finally you do it for money."

—*Molière (Jean-Baptiste Poquelin)*

"**B**eing a writer is like having homework every night for the rest of your life."

—*Lawrence Kasden*

"**Y**our manuscript is both good and original. But the part that is good is not original, and the part that is original is not good."

—*Attributed to Samuel Johnson, but probably apocryphal*

"**T**hose whose lot it is to ramble can seldom write, and those who know how to write very seldom ramble."

—*Samuel Johnson*

"**I**t's very hard to be a gentleman and a writer."

—*W. Somerset Maugham*

"**I**'ve always believed in writing without a collaborator, because where two people are writing the same book, each believes he gets all the worries and only half the royalties."

—*Agatha Christie*

"**S**ome editors are failed writers, but so are most writers."

—*T. S. Eliot*

"**T**he profession of book-writing makes horse-racing seem like a solid, stable business."

—*John Steinbeck*

"**W**hat no wife of a writer can ever understand is that a writer is working when he's staring out the window."

—*Rudolph Erich Rascoe*

"**W**ords are, of course, the most powerful drug used by mankind."

—*Rudyard Kipling*

"No iron can pierce the heart with such force as a period put at the right place."

—*Isaac Babel*

"The demonic paradox of writing: when you put something down that happened, people often don't believe it; whereas you can make up anything and people assume it must have happened to you."

—*Andrew Holleran*

"Getting even is one reason for writing."

—*William H. Gass*

"'Classic'—A book which people praise and don't read."

—*Mark Twain*

"All modern American literature comes from one book by Mark Twain called *Huckleberry Finn*."

—*Ernest Hemingway*

"If you want to get rich from writing, write the sort of thing that's read by persons who move their lips when they're reading to themselves."

—*Don Marquis*

"Writing is a form of therapy: sometimes I wonder how all those who do not write, compose, or paint can manage to escape the madness, melancholia, the panic and fear which are inherent in a human situation."

—*Graham Greene*

"Writing is the only thing that, when I do it, I don't feel as if I should be doing something else."

—*Gloria Steinem*

"I love being a writer. What I can't stand is the paperwork."

—*Peter De Vries*

"**T**here is no suffering comparable with that which a private person feels when he is for the first time pilloried in print."

—*Mark Twain*

"**N**ever read a book that is not a year old."

—*Ralph Waldo Emerson*

"**P**oetry is more worthy of serious attention than history."

—*Aristotle*

"**P**oetry is what gets lost in translation."

—*Robert Frost*

"**A** poet may do far more for a country than the owner of a nail factory."

—*Theodore Roosevelt*

"**W**riting free verse is like playing tennis without a net."

—*Robert Frost*

"**E**verywhere I go I'm asked if I think that university stifles writers. My opinion is that they don't stifle enough of them."

—*Flannery O'Connor*

nine

From Bad to Verse

"Poetry's a mere drug, sir."

—*George Farquhar*

"To say I'm a poet puts me in the company of versifiers, neontasters, fools, clods, and scoundrels masquerading as wise men."

—*Charles Bukowski,* poet

Two American presidents—Jimmy Carter and John Quincy Adams—have published volumes of poetry.

Pirate and tobacco monger Sir Walter Raleigh was also a renowned poet.

Versifier and recluse Emily Dickinson wouldn't show her poetry to family or friends. She was outraged and mortified when an acquaintance found her poetry stash and arranged to have seven of her poems published. It wasn't until four years after her death in 1886 that any more of her poems made their way into the light.

Dickinson did sometimes receive visitors, but she stayed in another room and listened to their conversations from there.

"**P**eople are exasperated by poetry which they do not understand and contemptuous of poetry which they understand without effort."

—*T. S. Eliot*

Do you know why a poet laureate is called that? The Greeks and Romans had a custom of crowning new officeholders with a wreath of laurel.

If you have a dream to become poet laureate, be aware that the competition is pretty steep, and you have to be willing to write poems commemorating holidays, retirements, and other mundane state occasions.

The first British poet laureate was John Dryden in 1670 (although Ben Jonson had performed the role without the title for Charles I in the sixty-three years prior to 1670). There have been only eighteen British laureates since then, because until recently the position was a lifetime appointment.

Notable British laureates include William Wordsworth, Ted Hughes, and Alfred, Lord Tennyson, who also served the longest— forty-two years, from 1850 to 1892.

The United States decided that if England had a poet laureate, it should have one too. Its first, Robert Penn Warren, was appointed on February 26, 1986, and there have been a total of nine since then.

Not just a playwright, Shakespeare also wrote 154 sonnets.

Or 152, if you believe the scholars who say that the last two were really written by somebody else. Shakespeare addressed his first 126 sonnets to a young nobleman. The next twenty-six are dedicated to a woman. The last two sonnets are not addressed to anybody.

Scholars and historians have not been able to identify either person. There is some evidence that the man was a financial patron and that the woman was a brunette with whom Shakespeare had an ambivalent yet passionate affair.

"Money is a kind of poetry."

—*Wallace Stevens, poet and insurance executive*

"There's no money in poetry, but there's also no poetry in money."

—*Poet laureate Robert Graves*

ten

By the Numbers

0: In Ireland zero percent is the rate of taxes on writers' income. In 1969, the Irish government wanted to nurture its local arts community instead of having its members move to London or America. They passed laws exempting all earnings from literary or artistic endeavors from income taxes.

0: The number of books Harper Lee wrote besides her bestseller, *To Kill a Mockingbird*.

0: The number of books that Margaret Mitchell wrote besides her bestseller, *Gone with the Wind*.

623 and 904: Barbara Cartland was a pretty prolific writer. Before her death in 2000, she had churned out 623 romance novels. However, South African writer Kathleen Lindsay (1903–1973) beat her soundly, having written 904 novels under six pen names.

37: The number of plays published by William Shakespeare.

16: The number of plays written by Neil Simon, the second-most-published playwright in the English language.

6 days: The amount of time it took Robert Lewis Stevenson to write the 60,000-word *Dr. Jekyll and Mr. Hyde.* That's an especially surprising output since he was suffering from the advanced stages of tuberculosis. On the other hand, he fortified his night-and-day writing with copious doses of cocaine.

100,000: That's the number of copies sold of *Naked Came the Stranger* by "Penelope Ashe"—actually twenty people who in 1969 were gathered by newspaperman Mike McGrady with the expressed purpose of writing the worst sex novel ever. "There

will be an unremitting emphasis on sex,"
wrote McGrady in his writers' guidelines.
"Also, true excellence in writing will be
blue-penciled into oblivion."

*3*10,000: The number of books and manuscripts about Shakespeare and his writing
in the Folger Shakespeare Library in Washington, D.C.

3,931: The total number of lines of dia-
logue in Shakespeare's longest play, *Hamlet.* It's more than twice as long as his
shortest, *A Comedy of Errors* (1,778 lines).

1,422: The number of lines an actor has to
learn in order to play the role of Hamlet.
The Danish prince's role hogs more than a
third of the play's total lines.

1,614: The most lines written by Shakespeare for one character. That character

was Sir John Falstaff, who appears in both *King Henry the Fourth* and *The Merry Wives of Windsor*.

Firsts

Aeschylus, known as the "father of Greek tragedies," wrote more than twice as many plays than Shakespeare—ninety in all. However, only seven of them have survived to present day.

The first known flashbacks in a literary work were in Homer's *Odyssey*, in which Odysseus tells his tale in the court of the Phoenicians.

Who invented the printed interview, with questions and answers transcribed verbatim? Some claim it was journalist Anne

Royall, who interviewed John Quincy
Adams in 1825.

The oldest known full novel is about a
thousand years old. It's *The Tale of Genji*,
written in Japan by a woman named
Murasaki Shikibu at the beginning of the
eleventh century.

The first poet among European settlers in
America was Anne Bradstreet of the Massachusetts Bay Colony.

The first novel written in America was *The
Power of Sympathy* written by William Hill
Brown in 1789. It was a juicy one, too, full
of seduction, rape, suicide, and incest.

Glory passes: Poet René Sully Prud-
homme won the very first Nobel Prize for
literature in 1901, but has since lapsed into
obscurity. He is not read much anymore,
not even in his native France.

The first woman to win a Pulitzer Prize was Edith Wharton. That was in 1921 for *The Age of Innocence*.

The first paperback book was reportedly an edition of *Faust* by Johann Wolfgang von Goethe, which went on sale in Germany in 1867.

The first female playwright in Europe was Hrosvitha, a nun who lived from A.D. 930 to 1002. She wrote six religious comedies, five of which were about sensual love.

eleven

You're My Inspiration

*S*tephen King says that reading *Dr. Doolittle* by Hugh Lofting as a child was what inspired him to want to become a writer.

When he needed a character name, Ian Fleming turned to his favorite bird-watching book, *Birds of the West Indies* by ornithologist James Bond.

Charles Dickens had a best friend named Bob Fagin. When Dickens needed a name for the scoundrel with a heart of gold, he named him Fagin. Whether his friend was honored or offended, we don't know.

Who says that all rock musicians are illiterate punks? Some are pretentious literary punks. Check out these band names that came from great (and not so great) literature:

- The Doors got their name from Aldous Huxley's *The Doors of Perception,* a book about experimenting with mescaline.

- William Burroughs's *Naked Lunch* inspired a host of rock names, including an industrial-rock band called (sensibly enough) Naked Lunch. Mama Cass Elliot and John Sebastian named an early folk-rock band the Mugwumps after creatures in the book that suckle humans with their reproductive juices. (Burroughs himself had borrowed the name from a nineteenth-century political movement.) And Steely Dan got its name from a giant metal dildo that appears in the book.

- *Naked Lunch* isn't the only Burroughs book that inspired a rock band. Soft Machine got its name from his book of the same name.

- Steppenwolf the band came from *Steppenwolf* the book by Hermann Hesse.

- Rock group Veruca Salt got its name from the spoiled rich girl in Roald Dahl's *Charlie and the Chocolate Factory.*

- Singer Tom Jones was a Welsh boy named Thomas John Woodward until a manager named him after the lusty character in Henry Fielding's novel of the same name.

- Ukulele player Tiny Tim and band Uriah Heep were both named after characters in Charles Dickens' novels.

- The 1960s skiffle band Mungo Jerry got its name from Mungojerrie, one of T. S. Eliot's *Practical Cats*.

- Manhattan Transfer was both a retro band and the name of a 1925 novel by John Dos Passos.

- Like the psychedelic band Moby Grape three decades earlier, the techno-master Moby got his name from Herman Melville's book about the white whale.

Of course, Moby's especially entitled—his real name is Richard Melville Hall, and he's the great-great-grandnephew of the author. On the other hand, he swears he's tried to read the book several times but has never been able to make it through to the end.

twelve

Kiddie Lit

American book publishers issue about 50,000 new books every year. Of these, about 5,000 are children's books.

Perhaps you know about *Chitty Chitty Bang Bang,* the children's book by spy writer Ian Fleming. But he's not the only writer for adults who dabbled in writing for a younger audience:

- Surrealist playwright Eugène Ionesco wrote two absurd children's stories: *Story Number One* and *The Endless Party.*

- Kurt Vonnegut wrote *Sun Moon Star* about the birth of Jesus.

- Donald Barthelme won the National Book Award only once, but not for his better-known serious writing. It was for his kid's book *The Slightly Irregular Fire Engine or The Hithering Thithering Djinn.*

- Good ol' boy William Faulkner wrote *The Wishing Tree.*

- Ken Kesey wrote *Little Tricker the Squirrel Meets Big Double the Bear.*

- Salman Rushdie wrote *Haroun and the Sea of Stories.*

- Virginia Woolf wrote *Nurse Lugton's Curtains.*

- Sylvia Plath wrote a cheery children's book called *The Bed Book* that was published after her suicide.

- Ever read *Daughter of the Tejas* by Ophelia Ray? Neither have we, but Ophelia was a pseudonym hiding the cowboy writer Larry McMurtry.

- Tough-guy detective writer Mickey Spillane wrote a novel for young readers called *The Day the Sea Rolled Back.*

- Popular novelist Anne Tyler wrote *Tumble Tower* with her daughter.

- John Updike borrowed from the Bard and wrote *Bottom's Dream,* a children's adaptation of *A Midsummer's Night Dream.*

- Gertrude Stein did her "rose is a rose is a rose" shtick for a younger crowd in *The World Is Round.*

- Oscar Wilde wrote a children's book called *The Happy Prince and Other Stories* in 1888 before his imprisonment knocked much of the whimsy out of him.

Some of the people we consider "children's authors" strongly resisted the title. A. A. Milne, for example, wished people would pay more attention to his serious adult plays than his Pooh Bear and friends.

Charles Dodgson wished people would pay more attention to his serious mathematics texts. He published under a pen name, Lewis Carroll, to avoid denting his professional dignity.

However, others were proud to wear the mantle. Ted "Dr. Seuss" Geisel once said about children, "You have 'em, I'll amuse 'em." Although married twice, he never had kids of his own.

Roald Dahl *(Charlie and the Chocolate Factory, James and the Giant Peach,* and others) started out as a British propaganda officer to America during World War II. After D-Day, he wrote war stories for a few years before finding his younger audience. He actually enjoyed that role, and even suggested to others that they should follow his lead. Kingsley Amis, novelist and poet, recounted in his *Memoirs* some advice that Dahl gave him at a dinner party—that he should write children's books: "That's where the money is today, believe me." Amis replied, "I couldn't do it. . . . I don't think I enjoyed children's books much when I was a child myself. I've got no feeling for that kind of thing." Responded Dahl, "Never mind, the little bastards'd swallow it anyway."

On a Golden Afternoon

Americans celebrated July 4, 1862, with a combination of patriotism and concern about war with the South. Thousands of miles away in England, however, math professor Charles Lutwidge Dodgson was rowing on the Isis River with the three young Liddell sisters, daughters of the dean of the Christ Church College of Oxford University. Alice, the youngest, got bored of the boat ride, so Dodgson told a tale featuring a girl named Alice. Afterward, he was urged to write it down, and so he did—it was, of course, *Alice's Adventures Underground.*

Although others have offered more elaborate explanations, L. Frank Baum himself said that he got the name for the Land of Oz from a filing cabinet marked "O–Z."

What's Good for Ma Goose

Was there really a Mother Goose? Nobody knows for sure. Some scholars say that she is based on a real person, but others say that she's completely fictional. Those who claim that Mother Goose existed split into at least three camps about who she was. Their theories are about as implausible as any fairy tale:

- One camp claims she was the Queen of Sheba from biblical times.

- Another theory suggests that Mother Goose was Queen Bertha, the mother of Charlemagne, the medieval military leader. This supposition is based on the fact that in her time Queen Bertha was known as "Queen Goose-Foot" and "Goose-Footed Bertha."

• A third theory proposes that there was an Elizabeth Goose (or Vergoose or Vertigoose), who lived in colonial Boston, and that her son-in-law, Thomas Fleet, collected her songs and rhymes and published them in 1719 as *Songs for the Nursery, or Mother Goose's Melodies.* Unfortunately there are serious problems with this theory. For one, no copy of this book has ever been found, and most scholars doubt it ever existed. For another, "Mother Goose" had already been known in French folk tales in the 1600s.

As far as anybody knows, the name "Mother Goose" first appeared in print in 1697. In that year, Charles Perrault, a French writer, published a book called *Histories: or Tales of Past Times, with Morals.* The front of the book pictured an old woman telling stories to three listeners in front of a fireplace. A sign above her read, *"Contes de Ma Mere L'Oye"* ("Mother Goose's Tales").

It was in this collection that the French folktales "Sleeping Beauty," "Red Riding Hood," and "Cinderella" first appeared in print.

Perrault's book was translated and published in England in 1729, including the old lady and the sign on the wall reading "Mother Goose's Tales." When it was reissued in 1768 by the John Newbery publishing house, the legend on the sign became the title. In 1781, Newbery also published *Mother Goose's Melody,* a collection of fifty-one rhymes including "Ding Dong, Bell," "Little Tom Tucker," and sixteen songs lifted from the plays of William Shakespeare.

The first Mother Goose book published in America seems to have been a reprint of Newbery's *Mother Goose's Melody,* published by Isaiah Thomas in 1786.

thirteen

Incognito

A number of scholars believe that William Shakespeare didn't always work alone: they say he collaborated with other dramatists, including John Fletcher, on a play called *The Two Noble Kinsmen*.

An unlikely detective writer was Gore Vidal, who wrote three mysteries in the early 1950s under the pseudonym "Edgar Box." His detective in all three books was one Peter Curler Sargeant II, a Harvard graduate who loved politics, the Hampton party scene, and ballet.

Brotherly Heights

Ever hear of the Bell brothers? No? Well, how about the Brontë sisters? In a time when it was considered unwomanly to write, the Brontës published their first writings under masculine pseudonyms:

"Currer Bell" (Charlotte Brontë), "Ellis Bell" (Emily Brontë), and "Acton Bell" (Anne Brontë).

The Brontës' first book was a collection of poems written by the three "Bell brothers" and published at the sisters' own expense. They sold only two copies.

The Bells did better, though, the next year. In 1847, Charlotte's *Jane Eyre,* Emily's *Wuthering Heights,* and Anne's *Agnes Grey* were all published under their masculine Bell pseudonyms.

The Brontë sisters' works were published just in time. In 1848, the same year Anne and Charlotte visited their publisher and revealed their true identities, Branwell, their brother, died of drug addiction and alcoholism. Anne died of tuberculosis, as did Emily the next year. Charlotte lasted another six years before dying of pneumonia.

Writers Onscreen

When directors adapt a recent literary work it has become a tradition to offer the writer of the work a bit part in the movie. This is partly because it's a little joke on the audience, but we suspect it's also because the cameo helps buy off the writer from complaining to the press later about how badly the story was adapted. If you want to see your favorite author on the screen, look quickly, because he or she is more likely to be playing "man in phone booth" than a major character. Here are some examples:

- Ann Beattie played the role of "waitress" in the movie *Head Over Heels* (based on her novel *Chilly Scenes of Winter*).

- James Dickey played "sheriff" in *Deliverance*.

- John Irving played "wrestling referee" in *The World According to Garp*.

- Jacqueline Susann played "first reporter" in *The Valley of the Dolls*.

- Jean Shepherd was the offscreen narrator of *A Christmas Story*.

- Likewise, Paul Bowles narrated *The Sheltering Sky* and Tom Robbins narrated *Even Cowgirls Get the Blues*.

- Charles Bukowski played "bar patron" in *Barfly*.

- Stephen King has showed up briefly in most of his book-based movies, including roles as "Jordy Verrill" in *Creepshow*, "minister" in *Pet Sematary*, and "man at Cashpoint" in *Maximum Overdrive*. (A little nepotism: His son Joseph King plays the comic book collector at the beginning of *Creepshow*.)

- Ian Fleming appeared as "man leaning on cane" in *From Russia with Love*.

- Arthur C. Clarke played "man on park bench" in *2010*.

- Peter Benchley played "reporter on beach" in *Jaws*.

- Kurt Vonnegut played "sad man on street" in *Mother Night* and "commercial director" in *Breakfast of Champions*.

Here's a different situation, where a writer threatened to sue to keep himself *off* the screen. Remember the James Earl Jones character in the movie *Field of Dreams?* In *Shoeless Joe,* the novella the movie was based on, the writer portrayed was not the fictitious grouch "Terrence Mann" but the genuine recluse J. D. Salinger. J. D. wasn't amused. Too bad, because it would've been fun to see the pitcher in the corn tossing fastballs to the catcher in the rye.

fourteen

Saints & Sinners, Quirks & Outrages

Novelist Édouard Corbière liked to build models of boats and then destroy them.

Sir A. Conan Doyle's detective Sherlock Holmes was the epitome of rationalism and logic. However, Doyle himself was not. He believed deeply in ghosts, fairies, and other spiritualistic claptrap, and was duped over and over again by charlatans and hoaxers.

Lord Byron became paranoid about assorted enemies and often carried a loaded pistol.

Percy Shelley suffered from recurring hallucinations that involved being stalked by a deranged gunman. Perhaps it was Lord Byron?

Take a good look at your writing—would reading it aloud in a court of law prove your sanity? That was what Sophocles had to face when his sons tried to have the ninety-year-old playwright declared mentally incompetent. Sophocles defended himself by reading passages from *Oedipus at Colonus,* his newest play (coincidentally, it was about patricide). The judge chastised Sophocles' sons and declared the playwright sane.

Add to the list of jailhouse writers the apostle Paul, who wrote a good chunk of the Bible's New Testament from his jail cell.

You may know him for the *Forsyte Saga,* but John Galsworthy was most interested in using his work to push along social progress. His commitment to his craft was such that in 1910 he shed his famous name, dressed as a beggar, and threw a brick through a display window in order to get arrested. From his six months as a poor person in jail, much of it in solitary confinement, Galsworthy wrote a play called *Justice*, which led to the reform of England's prison system.

We could go on and on about the FBI's surveillance of American intellectuals. However, here are some excerpts from FBI files about a few of our favorite authors:

- Allen Ginsberg: "Emotionally unstable . . . potentially dangerous"

- Dorothy Parker: "Member of the League of Women Shoppers"

- Tennessee Williams: "Has the reputation of being a homosexual"

- Sinclair Lewis: "Writes propaganda for accepting the Negro as a social equal"

When young Henry David Thoreau graduated from Harvard, he refused to take his diploma. "It isn't worth five dollars," he said, complaining that Harvard taught "all the branches of learning, but none of the roots."

Like George Sands before her, poet Amy Lowell enjoyed a good cigar as she worked. In 1915, fearing wartime shortages, she bought 10,000 of her favorite Manilans.

You'd think campy, floridly outrageous Oscar Wilde would be given a hard time in America's Old West. Not true. He found a rapt audience in many small towns and camps during a yearlong speaking tour that covered 30,000 miles and thirty-four states and territories. He thoroughly charmed the rough-and-tumble miners in Leadville, Colorado. Afterward he wrote, "They were polished and refined compared to the people I met in larger cities back East."

Children's author Margaret Wise Brown, who wrote many a tender kitty-and-bunny tale like *Goodnight Moon* and *The Bunny's*

Birthday, loved to hunt rabbits. She collected their severed feet as trophies.

When San Francisco's Board of Supervisors voted to limit the number of street parking permits per city household to four, author Danielle Steele—who had somehow amassed twenty-six spots around her palatial Pacific Heights mansion, to the consternation of her neighbors—fired off a dramatic protest to the local paper: "I am not deserving of either the harsh, unkind judgments, nor the abuse directed at me as a result of people's jealousy, although it is not unfamiliar to me, nor others like me." She added that as a result of the controversy, she and her eight children have been "terrorized by hostile press and angry people at our gate."

Art lovers and historians were absolutely appalled when crime writer Patricia Cornwall, obsessed with proving that artist

Walter Richard Sickert was Jack the Ripper, bought up thirty of Sickert's paintings for as much as $70,000 each, tearing some of them to shreds looking for clues.

A former FBI agent blamed his wife's affair with Patricia Cornwall for driving him over the edge. He was tried in 1996 for kidnapping a minister to lure his wife to a church that had been booby-trapped with dynamite (and Play-Doh molded to look like dynamite). He was sentenced to sixty-one years in jail, but that was knocked down to twenty-eight years on appeal.

The Marquis de Sade, father of sadism, had a lot of prison time to write. After a stint in the army, he spent twenty-seven years locked up for various sexual offenses and died in an insane asylum. Many of de Sade's books were considered so obscene that they weren't published until the 1950s, a century and a half after his death.

When poet and painter William Blake was a child, he swore that he saw the prophet Ezekiel in a tree in the family garden. Blake was afflicted and blessed with eidetic vision, a condition that allowed him to view memories, mental musings, and hallucinations with a photographic clarity.

John Keats had public fits of alternately weeping and laughing.

Author and critic Edmund Wilson didn't bother to file income tax returns from 1946 to 1955. Oops!

Here's a doozy from the writers hall of shame. When English author William Beckford wrote his novel *The History of the Caliph Vathek* in French, he modeled his caliph on himself and tried to live the part. The wealthiest man in England, Beckford designed his own mammoth castle, which he ruled with a ten-year-old boyfriend and stocked with dwarves as servants, a harem of boys, and his own militia to keep outsiders from intruding.

Statistics from *Scientific American* from 1995 indicate that writers and artists are ten times more likely to suffer from clinical depression than members of the general population. Writers' incidence of suicide may be as much as eighteen times higher.

Saints Preserve Us

Here is evidence of how hard a writer's life is, or at least how much a writer needs divine intervention. While most professions only have one patron saint in the Catholic Church, writers have *four:* Saints Lucy, Frances de Sales, John the Apostle, and

Paul the Apostle (but not the apostles George and Ringo). But that's just the beginning.

- Advertising and public relations writers are protected by Saint Bernadine of Siena.

- Television writers can get guidance and support from Saint Clare of Assisi.

- Religious writers, from Saint Peter Canisius.

- Editors can appeal to Saint John Bosco for help and comfort on deadlines.

- Publishers are protected by Saints James Duckett and Thomas Aquinas.

- Poets can depend on Saints Cecilia and David. *Spanish* poets are specifically represented by John of the Cross.

- Printers may appeal to Saint Augustine of Hippo for any of their problems, but if there's a specific problem with your printing press (or ink-jet printer, for that matter) try Saint Brigid of Ireland.

Other useful saints for writers:

- Isadore of Seville, patron saint of computer users

- Eugene de Mazenod, patron saint of dysfunctional families

- Maximillian Kolbe, the patron saint of substance abusers

- Saint Joseph, patron saint of people in doubt

- Jude Thaddeus, patron saint of desperate and impossible situations

- Fiacre, patron saint of hemorrhoids

- Agostina Pietrantoni, protector against sinking into poverty

- Catherine of Alexandria, patron saint of libraries

- Gotteschalk, patron saint of linguists

- Rita of Cascia, protector against loneliness

- Christina the Astonishing, protector against insanity

- Ursicinus of Saint-Ursanne, patron saint of stiff necks
- Amalburga, protector against carpal tunnel syndrome
- Drogo, patron saint of unattractive people
- Expiditus, protector against procrastination
- Quirinus, patron saint of the obsessed

fifteen

"Easy Reading Is Damned Hard Writing"

"A good title is apt, specific, attractive, new, and short."

—*W. Somerset Maugham*

"Writing is not a profession but a vocation of unhappiness."

—*Georges Simenon*

"No one ever committed suicide while reading a good book, but many have tried while trying to write one."

—*Robert Byrne*

"An absolutely necessary part of a writer's equipment, almost as necessary as talent, is the ability to stand up under punishment, both the punishment the world hands out and the punishment he inflicts upon himself."

—*Irwin Shaw*

"**Y**our life story would not make a good book. Don't even try."

—*Fran Liebowitz*

"**W**riters have two main problems. One is writer's block, when the words won't come at all, and the other is logorrhea, when the words come so fast that they can hardly get to the wastebasket in time."

—*Cecilia Bartholomew*

"**A**ny writer, I suppose, feels that the world into which he was born is nothing less than a conspiracy against the cultivation of his talent."

—*James Baldwin*

"**I**f you would not be forgotten as soon as you are dead and rotten, either write things worth reading, or do things worth the writing."

—*Benjamin Franklin*

"**T**he road to hell is paved with adverbs."

—*Mark Twain*

"**E**asy reading is damned hard writing."

—*Nathaniel Hawthorne*

"**I**f writing were easy, everyone would be doing it."

—*Andy Rooney*

"**T**he art of writing is the art of applying the seat of the pants to the seat of the chair."

—*Mary Heaton Vorse*

"**G**ood work doesn't happen with inspiration. It comes with constant, often tedious and deliberate effort. If your vision of a writer involves sitting in a café, sipping an aperitif with one's fellow geniuses, become a drunk. It's easier and far less exhausting."

—*William Hefferman*

"**I** get a fine warm feeling when I'm doing well, but that pleasure is pretty much negated by the pain of getting started each day. Let's face it, writing is hell."

—*William Styron*

"**Y**ou need a certain amount of nerve to be a writer."

—*Margaret Atwood*

"**W**riting energy is like anything else: The more you put in, the more you get out."

—*Richard Reeves*

"**T**here is no perfect time to write. There's only now."

—*Barbara Kingsolver*

"**I**f the writer has a masterpiece within, he had better save it on paper. Otherwise, none of us will ever miss it."

—*Steve Martini*

"When I start a book, I always think it's patently absurd that I can write one. No one, certainly not me, can write a book 500 pages long. But I know I can write 15 pages, and if I write 15 pages every day, eventually I will have 500 of them."

—*John Saul*

"Writing a novel is like driving a car at night. You can see only as far as your headlights, but you can make the whole trip that way."

—*E. L. Doctorow*

"Good writers are those who keep the language efficient. That is to say, keep it accurate, keep it clear."

—*Ezra Pound*

"No tears in the writer, no tears in the reader. No surprise in the writer, no surprise in the reader."

—*Robert Frost*

"**O**nly a mediocre writer is always at his best."

—*W. Somerset Maugham*

"**W**hat I adore is supreme professionalism. I'm bored by writers who can write only when it's raining."

—*Noel Coward*

"**T**here are three rules for writing a novel. Unfortunately, no one knows what they are."

—*W. Somerset Maugham*

"**T**he most valuable writing habit I have is not to answer questions about my writing habits."

—*Christopher Morley*

"**W**riting is easy. You just sit down at the typewriter and open a vein."

—*Red Smith*

"**A** writer is someone for whom writing is more difficult than it is for other people."

—*Thomas Mann*

"**N**o good novel will ever proceed from a superficial mind."

—*Henry James*

"**T**hree hours a day will produce as much as a man ought to write."

—*Anthony Trollope*

"**L**earn to write well, or not to write at all."

John Sheffield

"**T**he difference between the right word and the almost right word is the difference between lightning and the lightning bug."

—*Mark Twain*

"**W**hen in doubt, have two guys come through the door with guns."

—*Raymond Chandler*

"**A** man may write at any time, if he will set himself doggedly to it."

—*Samuel Johnson*

"**If** writers were good businessmen, they'd have too much sense to be writers."

—*Irving S. Cobb*

"**An** author who speaks about his own books is almost as bad as a mother who talks about her own children."

—*Benjamin Disraeli*

"**What** is written without effort is in general read without pleasure."

—*Samuel Johnson*

"**The** only sensible ends of literature are, first the pleasurable toil of writing; second, the gratification of one's family and friends; and lastly, the solid cash."

—*Nathaniel Hawthorne*

Rewriting

"**As** a general rule, run a pen through every other word you have written; you have no idea what vigor it will give your style."

—*Sydney Smith*

"**When** rewriting, move quickly. It's a little like cutting your own hair."

—*Robert Stone*

"**I** have rewritten—often several times— every word I have ever written. My pencils outlast their erasers."

—*Vladimir Nabokov*

"**I** have never thought of myself as a good writer. Anyone who wants reassurance of that should read one of my first drafts. But I'm one of the world's great rewriters."

—*James Michener*

"**I**t is perfectly okay to write garbage—as long as you edit brilliantly."

—*C. J. Cherryh*

"**H**alf of my life is an act of revision."

—*John Irving*

"**W**hat I had to face, the very bitter lesson that everyone who wants to write has got to learn, was that a thing may in itself be the finest piece of writing one has ever, done, and yet have absolutely no place in the manuscript one hopes to publish."

—*Thomas Wolfe*

"**R**ewriting is like scrubbing the basement floor with a toothbrush."

—*Pete Murphy*

"**T**here are days when the result is so bad that no fewer than five revisions are required. In contrast, when I'm greatly inspired, only four revisions are needed."

—John Kenneth Galbraith

"There is a difference between a book of two hundred pages from the very beginning, and a book of two hundred pages which is the result of an original eight hundred pages. The six hundred are there. Only you don't see them."

—Elie Wiesel

"The beautiful part of writing is that you don't have to get it right the first time unlike, say, a brain surgeon."

—Robert Cormier

Give 'em the Business

"At first, editors will reject everything. What you do is keep sending the same poems to the same people, after a decent interval, of course. After about the fourth or fifth time, they will actually have read them, and they will hear a little bell ring that they'll call the shock of recognition, and they'll take one."

—*Richard Palmer Blackmuir*

"I object to publishers: the one service they have done me is to teach me to do without them. They combine commercial rascality with artistic touchiness and pettishness, without being either good businessmen or fine judges of literature. All that is necessary in the production of a book is an author and a bookseller, without the intermediate parasite."

—*George Bernard Shaw*

"**O**ne should fight like the devil the temptation to think well of editors. They are all, without exception—at least some of the time—incompetent or crazy. By the nature of their profession they read too much, with the result that they grow jaded and cannot recognize talent though it dances in front of their eyes."

—*John Gardner*

"**A**n editor should have a pimp for a brother so he'd have someone to look up to."

—*Gene Fowler*

"**A**s difficult as it is for a writer to find a publisher—admittedly a daunting task—it is twice as difficult for a publisher to sort through the chaff, select the wheat, and profitably publish a worthy list."

—*Olivia Goldsmith*

Jack London On Writing

- Don't quit your job in order to write unless there is none dependent upon you.

- Don't dash off a six-thousand word story before breakfast.

- Don't write too much. Concentrate your sweat on one story rather than dissipate it over a dozen.

- Don't loaf and invite inspiration: light out after it with a club, and if you don't get it you will nonetheless get something that looks remarkably like it.

- Set yourself a "stint," and see that you do that "stint" every day.

- Study the tricks of the writers who have arrived. They have mastered the tools with which you are cutting your fingers.

- Keep a notebook. Travel with it, eat with it, sleep with it. Slap into it every stray thought that flutters up into your brain. Cheap paper is less perishable than gray matter, and lead pencil markings endure longer than memory.

- And work. Find out about this earth, this universe. . . .

—*From article, "Getting into Print," 1903*

sixteen

A Word's Worth

The term *freelancing* dates from the twelfth century, when knights who lost employment with royal houses offered themselves as mercenaries.

Lewis Carroll contributed the word *chortle* (combining "chuckle" and "snort") to the English language from his poem "Jabberwocky." The new word from a two-word combo is called a *portmanteau* word, taking its name from the French word for a double-compartment suitcase. More common examples include *smog* ("smoke" and "fog"), *brunch* ("breakfast" with "lunch"), and *breathalyzer* ("breath" and "analyzer").

William Shakespeare was a genius, no doubt about it. But let's not overdo the praise. Some fans claim he coined as many as 10,000 words, including *alligator, assassination, bump, eventful, lonely, pander, leapfrog, skim milk,* and *hobnob.* However, that doesn't make any sense—if he really coined words en masse his audience probably wouldn't have been able to understand his plays. More likely the words were already being used in conversation, and he's merely the earliest known writer to have put them to paper.

Before Noah Webster compiled his dictionary of renown in 1806, he first wrote a spelling book and a grammar book. They were bestsellers too—schools bought more than 100 million copies of the spelling book during the nineteenth century.

Webster single-handedly spent more than twenty years researching in England, France, and the United States to find the root origins of many of the 70,000 words that appeared in his first dictionary.

Webster is responsible for changing the way we spell several words. Take *music,* for instance. The original spelling was *musick,* but Webster thought the *k* was too redundant when he wrote his dictionary. He changed *plough* to *plow,* removed the *u*'s from *colour* and *honour,* and turned *centre* into *center.* His dictionary also changed the pronunciation of "tion" from "she-un" to "shun."

Facetiously is the only English word we know that uses all the vowels (and part-time vowel *y)* in proper order.

The oldest still-existing letter is *o,* first used by the Egyptians in about 3000 B.C.

The newest letters are *j* and *v. J* was derived from *i* in about 1600. See any monuments with words like "TRVTH"? *V* had double duty as vowel and consonant until someone got the bright idea to make round the bottom and create a separate letter, *u.* This happened during the Renaissance.

The most frequently used letters of the alphabet are (in order of frequency) *e, t, o, a,* and *n*.

Think of what a difficulty it would be if you couldn't use the most common letter in your writing. In 1937, Ernest Vincent Wright took the challenge head on and wrote a book called *Gadsby, A Story of Over 50,000 Words Without Using the Letter "E."* He literally tied down the *e* key on his typewriter and spent 165 days writing without *e*'s (the *e*-filled subtitle was added later by the publisher). Not that Wright lived a life of ease from his *e*-less accomplishment: He died the day *Gadsby* was published.

Competent writers know that *e.g.* means "for example" and *i.e.* means "that is" and never confuse the two in their writing. However it's a sure bet that few know that the abbreviations stand for *exempli gratia* and *id est*.

Et al. is an abbreviation, but it hardly seems worth bothering, since it saves only two letters. It stands for *et alia* ("and other things") or *et alii* ("and other people"), making it more specific than *et cetera* ("and the rest").

A Mrs. Malaprop was a comical character in Richard Brinsley Sheridan's 1775 play, *The Rivals*. She managed to mangle the language in an entertaining way. One of her lines was, "Sure, if I reprehend anything in this world it is the use of my oracular tongue, and a nice derangement of epitaphs!" A number of comic characters from Amos and Andy to Archie Bunker have used the same shtick, but the term *malaprop* for such things still applies.

Italian scientist Girolamo Fracastoro was a poet as well as a physician. In 1530, he wrote a poem called "Syphilis" about a shepherd infected with the disease. Syphilus was the shepherd's name, and the poem was popular enough that the affliction came to be known as "Syphilis's disease," and then just "syphilis." Before that, it was called *morbus gallicus* ("the disease of the French").

Wuther is an obscure word referring to the noise that wind makes blowing through trees, which is why *Wuthering Heights* is called that.

The word *robot* was coined in 1921 by Czech writer Karel Çapek for a play called *R. U. R.* ("Rossum's Universal Robots"). He constructed the term from a Czech root word meaning "working."

Pandemonium now, of course, means any hellishly chaotic place. In *Paradise Lost,* John Milton invented "Pandemonium" as the home of Satan and friends. The word comes from the Latin and means "a place for all demons."

Utopia was a word invented by Sir Thomas More, whose martyrdom was recounted in *A Man for All Seasons*. His 1516 novel, *Utopia,* was about a fictitious paradise supposedly found in the New World. In Latin, the word is a pun on both "good place" and "no place."

Some claim that headline writers as a professional group have coined a disproportionate number of words. Not surprisingly, given the space limitations of their art form, most of the words are shortened versions of longer words. Credit them with such words as *flu, veep, A-bomb, polio, quake, prof,* and *champ.*

Credit Norman Mailer with coining the word *factoid* in his 1973 book *Marilyn.* However, the popular meaning has shifted a bit since his first definition: "Facts which have no existence before appearing in a magazine or newspaper, creations which are not so much lies as a product to manipulate emotion in the Silent Majority."

Do you know Charles E. Willer? Probably not, but there's a good chance you've typed his words. Willer, a court reporter, was a friend of typewriter inventor Christopher Latham, and he created a phrase of common letter combinations to help Latham test his keyboards. The phrase was, "Now is the time for all good men to come to the aid of their party."

The funny thing about Willer's phrase is that it isn't a *pangram*—that is, a sentence using all the letters of the alphabet. Good short pangrams include "Pack my box with five dozen liquor jugs" and the more famous "The quick brown fox jumped over lazy dogs."

Place Names

Legend has it that Tarzana, California, was named after Tarzan. Actually the reverse is true. Edgar Rice Burroughs owned fifty acres near the town, and when he was casting about for a name for his ape-man, he decided "Tarzan" would do.

Was Zanesville, Ohio, named after Zane Grey, the native-son Western writer? No such luck—both city and author were named after the town's founder, Ebenezer Zane.

"Reading Jail" sounds like a great retreat for a lover of literature. However, don't be misled. The "gaol" in Reading, Berkshire, in England was where Oscar Wilde was sent for "unnatural practices" (homosexuality), and despite the name, very little reading was done there.

seventeen

Random Facts from the Bibliophiles

"**A** man's library is a sort of harem."

—*Ralph Waldo Emerson*

Here's another good reason for having your home lined with books: According to the United States Federal Emergency Management Agency (FEMA), fourteen inches of books and magazines will protect you from nuclear radiation just as well as four inches of concrete.

How sexually repressed were the Victorians? Well, *Lady Gough's Book of Etiquette,* an advice book from the time, strictly forbids allowing the books of male authors to lie alongside those of "authoresses" on bookshelves. There was one exception: The books of married writers such as Mary Shelley and Percy Bysshe Shelley could be placed together.

"**M**y friends may not be good in mathematics, but they are excellent book keepers."

—*Sir Walter Scott, speaking about books lent but never returned*

The Bible is actually a collection of sixty-six books written over 1,500 years by forty-four authors. It wasn't originally divided into chapters and verses. Stephan Langton came up with the chapters in A.D. 1228; the verses were numbered in 1448 (Old Testament) and 1551 (New Testament).

"**A**ll books are either dreams or swords. You can cut or you can drug with words."

—*Amy Lowell*

"**I** always read the last page of a book first so that if I die before I finish I'll know how it turned out."

—*Nora Ephron*

According to researchers, women readers are four times more likely than men to read the last page of a book first, and twice as likely to skip pages and jump ahead in the story.

Researchers from the University of Wales lurking around libraries found that fiction readers had the strangest dreams. Fantasy fans had more nightmares and more dreams in which they were aware they were dreaming. Romance novel writers' dreams were the most emotionally intense. And children who read scary books were three times more likely to have nightmares.

The Dewey Decimal System is used by 95 percent of all public and school libraries in the United States. However, most colleges and universities use the Library of Congress System.

"**O**ften while reading a book one feels that the author would have preferred to paint rather than write; one can sense the pleasure he derives from describing a landscape or a person, as if he were painting what he is saying, because deep in his heart he would have preferred to use brushes and colors."

—*Pablo Picasso*

"**T**he paperback is very interesting but I find it will never replace the hardcover book—it makes a very poor doorstop."

—*Alfred Hitchcock*

The Bulwer-Lytton Bad Writing Contest

Are you a divinely inspired terrible writer? Perhaps you should send in an entry to the Bulwer-Lytton Fiction Contest, a celebration of wretched opening lines of fictitious novels sponsored each year by the San Jose State University English Department.

The contest was named after Edward George Bulwer-Lytton, a Victorian writer who was responsible for "The pen is mightier than the sword," and "The great unwashed." His best-known work is probably *The Last Days of Pompeii*.

However, that isn't why he was "honored" with this contest. You can indirectly blame the contest on Snoopy. The comic strip dog repeatedly wrote novels that began, "It was a dark and stormy night." Scott Rice, a graduate student, took it upon himself to try to discover the original source that Snoopy had plagiarized. He not only uncovered the source, but found it within a really bad opening line in Bulwer-Lytton's novel *Paul Clifford:*

> It was a dark and stormy night; the rain fell in torrents—except at occasional intervals, when it was checked by a violent gust of wind which swept up the streets (for it is in London that our scene lies), rattling along the housetops, and fiercely agitating the scanty flame of the lamps that struggled against the darkness.

After Rice graduated and became a professor, he was often drafted to judge literary contests. The quality of the writing and the odd standards by which they were being judged were such that he decided that they were, in effect, "bad writing contests but with prolix, overlong, and generally lengthy submissions." Rice decided to streamline the process and create a contest for deliberately bad writing consisting of no more than a single opening sentence.

The first Bulwer-Lytton contest in 1982 attracted only three entries. Nowadays, though, more than 10,000 people submit entries in a dozen categories. (You can read this year's winners and submit your own efforts for the next via the Internet at *www.bulwer-lytton.com*.)

Sleuthing from the Grave

Sherlock Holmes died in 1893 ... but then came back to life ten years later. After writing twenty-four Holmes stories in six years, Sir A. Conan Doyle had grown weary of the popular hero and wanted to focus on writing historical novels. So he figured he could put an end to the whole thing by having Holmes plunge to his death from Switzerland's Reichenbach Falls, holding his archenemy, Professor Moriarty, in a mutual death grip.

Although public outcry was enormous, Doyle remained adamant about not bringing Holmes back. Ten years later, though, *McClure's* magazine in the United States offered Doyle $5,000 per story if he'd bring his detective back to life. That was the equivalent of nearly $100,000 in today's money, and Doyle couldn't resist. His first story had him coming out of hiding after ten years, and Doyle wrote Holmes stories for a quarter-century before retiring himself and his detective for good in 1927.

Holmes still receives letters at his fictional home at 221B Baker Street from people around the world, some of whom are trying to enlist his help in solving crimes.

Doyle apparently had scouted out the location well. According to the Sherlock Holmes Museum, which now occupies 221B Baker Street, city records show that the house was a lodging house between 1860 and 1934, and that some of the maids who worked there were related to a man named Holmes. A Doctor Watson lived next door in the 1890s. He made false teeth.

Biblio Bloopers

Like some other prominent writers, Miguel de Cervantes had some difficulties with keeping his story straight. In one chapter of *Don Quixote*, Sancho Panza sells his donkey, but before long is somehow riding it again. In other parts of the book, his wallet, food, and helmet are lost or destroyed, yet each reappear later in the story without explanation.

Daniel Defoe had a similar problem with Robinson Crusoe. The shipwrecked sailor strips off his clothes before swimming back to his ruined ship to salvage what he can. Once there the naked sailor finds that some provisions are still good, and so "being very well disposed to eat, I went to the bread room and filled my pockets with biscuit." (A naked sailor swimming with biscuits in his pockets intending to somehow keep them dry is something we don't even want to think about.)

O. Henry (William Sydney Porter) made an even more telling error in "The Gift of the Magi," his most famous short story. Porter had begun writing brilliant short stories while serving time in prison. While the courts had ruled that Porter willfully embezzled from his day job as a bank teller, his defenders claimed that, like many writers, he was just not very good with money. There is some support for that claim: In the first lines of "Magi," he described an impossible set of change: "One dollar and eighty-seven cents. That was all. And 60 cents of it was in pennies. . . ."

Miscellany

Thanks to his former trade, making pencils in his father's factory, Henry David Thoreau impressed his friends with this trick: He could plunge his hands into a barrel of loose pencils and emerge with an even dozen in each hand.

History also records that Thoreau was an excellent figure skater.

Norman Mailer was one of the cofounders of the *Village Voice*.

Upton Sinclair began writing professionally at age fifteen. He turned out 8,000 words a day, seven days a week, by dictating to a stenographer. In eighteen months from June 1897 to November 1898—a time when he passed from age nineteen to twenty and was a taking a full academic load as a graduate student at Columbia University—he found the time to publish magazine articles totaling 1,275,000 words.

The Lord of the Rings was supposed to be a single book, but J. R. R. Tolkien's publisher unilaterally decided to turn it into a trilogy. Tolkien was not pleased with that decision, and complained loud and long about it to anybody who would listen.

Although he wrote eighty-two Perry Mason books, that wasn't Erle Stanley Gardner's only book line. Fictitious district attorney Douglas Selby starred in nine of his novels. Under the pen name A. A. Fair, Gardner produced twenty-nine books about private eyes Bertha Cool and Donald Lam. Gardner also wrote nonfiction books and hundreds of western and science fiction short stories and novelettes.

British poet John Milton wrote *Paradise Lost* after he became completely blind at age forty-five.

Voltaire and the Marquis de Sade were each the same height as Mickey Rooney—5 foot 3 inches.

Redheaded writers include William Shakespeare, George Bernard Shaw, Emily Dickinson, Mark Twain, and Sinclair Lewis.

The richest author is Stephen King, whose personal fortune has been estimated at more than $84 million.

However, the most successful author was Agatha Christie. Her seventy-eight mystery novels have sold more than 2 billion copies.

Katherine Anne Porter took twenty years to write *Ship of Fools*.

Isaac Asimov wrote or cowrote 300 books on a variety of subjects. However, despite literary legend, he does not have a book in each of the ten major categories of the Dewey Decimal System—he missed Philosophy/Psychology (100–199).

You're never too young or old, apparently. First-published authors we know of range in age from four (Dorothy Straight, author of *How the World Began*) to 102 (Alice Pollack, author of *Portrait of My Victorian Youth*).

Poet Robert Burns was fed up with poverty in his native Scotland, and in 1786 decided to emigrate to the British colony of Jamaica. Only one problem—he didn't have the money for transportation. Figuring some poetry lovers might have some pity on him, he began selling a thin volume of his poems that he'd self-published. To his surprise, the collection became a resounding success, and he became so busy and wealthy republishing new editions, he didn't have time or reason to go to Jamaica. So he stuck around and became Scotland's national poet instead.

Why did William Shakespeare include comic characters even in his most violent tragedies? You can credit his genius for the dramatic effect of comic relief, but you also have to take into account that acting companies needed plays that would provide roles for all their major performers. Many of Shakespeare's scenes—for example, the grave diggers in *Hamlet*—were included simply to give the company's leading comic actor a role in the production.

Why do Shakespeare's plays go so blasted long? How could people standing in the theater make it through a production that ran nearly four hours? Well, in Shakespeare's time, the plays weren't that long because actors spoke their lines more quickly, using a clear speaking style that carried well in the small theaters. Nowadays, with larger auditoriums—and since the 400-year-old language is harder for audiences to understand—actors have to slow their delivery, significantly lengthening the plays.

Mystery writer Mary Roberts Rinehart was nothing if not prolific. In 1903, she published her first short story. Before the year was out she had published forty-four more.

When Ray Bradbury began writing, he didn't own a typewriter. He wrote *Fahrenheit 451* (1953) in the basement of UCLA's library, where you could rent time on a typewriter for 10¢ an hour. His first draft was titled *The Fire Man,* and the typewriter time cost him $9.80 (about $63 in today's money).

Mary Shelley was nineteen when she and her husband, poet Percy Bysshe Shelley, went for a weekend in Geneva with a few friends, including Lord Byron. To fill the long rainy nights, the writerly crowd challenged each other to come up with ghost stories. Then and there, Ms. Shelley came up with the story of Dr. Frankenstein and his intelligent, articulate creature. Her fellow travelers urged her to expand the story to a novel's length, and the rest is history.

You of course know that Frankenstein is the doctor, not the monster (who remains unnamed through the book).

Shelley's book's full title is *Frankenstein: The Modern Prometheus*. Prometheus, you might remember from Greek mythology, was the god who gave the secret of fire to humanity. As punishment, Zeus chained him to the Caucasus Mountains and visited him in the form of an eagle to eat Prometheus' liver every day for eternity.

A lot of people have tried their hands at detective stories. Some you might not have suspected include Pearl S. Buck, George Bernard Shaw, and two American presidents: Abraham Lincoln and Franklin Roosevelt.

Chairman Mao's *Little Red Book* was a huge seller in scores of languages. But few people know that Mao was an accomplished poet as well. So was Vietnam's Ho Chi Minh.

Would Americans ever elect a writer to office? Doesn't happen often—actors and professional wrestlers have a better chance. Still, Gore Vidal, Norman Mailer, William Buckley, Jimmy Breslin, John Greenleaf Whittier, Jack London, Upton Sinclair, James Michener, and Hunter S. Thompson have all thrown their hats into the ring as candidates for offices. Not one of them won.

eighteen

The End

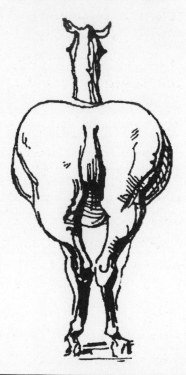

Greek playwright Aeschylus reportedly died of a skull fracture after an eagle, mistaking the playwright's glistening white dome for a rock, dropped a turtle or oyster on his bald head to crack it open.

The Greek poet Terpander (c. 712–c. 645 B.C.) died when someone threw a fig at him as he was singing a song. It flew into his mouth and lodged in his windpipe.

When Walt Whitman died, his brain was put in a jar and donated to the University of Pennsylvania. They don't have it any more—a lab technician dropped the jar on the floor and damaged the brain. The university quietly discarded it, and his "Specimen Days" were over.

French playwright Molière was also an actor. One night, though desperately ill, he decided the show must go on. When the performance ended, he collapsed and had to be carried home. Once there, a blood vessel broke in his throat, and the curtain closed on his last act.

Edgar Allan Poe accidentally drank himself to death by systematically stumbling into various Baltimore polling places and repeatedly casting ballots in order to get the free voting-day drinks traditionally offered at the time. His fiancée was heartbroken.

Mark Twain was born in the year of Halley's Comet, and, fulfilling his own prophecy, he died the next time it cycled near the Earth seventy-six years later.

Hans Christian Andersen was deathly afraid of being buried alive, so he left notes around his bed saying that he only "seemed dead."

No happy returns: The day Shakespeare died happened to be his fifty-second birthday. It was also the same year that Cervantes died.

Voltaire's body was stolen in 1814 from the Pantheon in Paris by a group of right-wing religious extremists and dumped in a garbage heap somewhere. This wasn't discovered for more than fifty years. The memorial in the Pantheon remains, but his sarcophagus is but an empty shell.

Before Voltaire's burial, his heart and brain had been removed. His brain was auctioned off in the late 1800s and has since disappeared. Last time anybody checked, his heart is in the Bibliotheque Nationale ... we hope under a decent lock and key.

Thomas Hardy's heart likewise was kept apart when his body was cremated. The idea was to bury it in Stinsford, England, the home of his beloved childhood church, and home to the family plot. All was going according to plan until his sister's cat leaped up onto her kitchen table, snatched the heart, and ran off into the woods with it.

Writers Plot Their Last Chapters

Existentialist Albert Camus wrote, "There is but one truly serious philosophical problem and that is suicide." Writers are used to being able to determine the fates of their characters, so it's not too surprising that they're tempted to do the same with their own lives. They each wrote their personal endings a little differently. For instance:

- Sylvia Plath stuck her head into an unlit gas oven.

- Ernest Hemingway put a shotgun to his head.

- Virginia Woolf filled her pockets with rocks and walked into the Ouse River after leaving two different drafts of a suicide note.

- Poet Anne Sexton went into her garage, started her car, and died of carbon monoxide poisoning.

- Author Stefan Zweig and his wife Elisabeth injected themselves with a mix of barbiturates and ant poison.

- Jack London killed himself, perhaps accidentally, with an overdose of morphine at the age of forty.

- According to legend, Li Po, China's most honored poet, died in A.D. 762 while drunkenly trying to grasp the reflection of the moon in the still waters of a lake.

- Simone Weil starved herself to death in London while demonstrating against the Nazis occupation of France. She had allowed herself to eat only the same amount of food the Nazis were rationing to each citizen of France at the time.

- British poet Charlotte Mew killed herself by drinking disinfectant.

- John Berryman leaped to his death from a bridge in Mississippi. On his way down, he waved a casual good-bye to a passerby.

- Hart Crane had a similarly cheery end. On a ship crowded with passengers, he shouted "Good-bye, everybody!" and leapt over the rail.

- Pulitzer Prize-winning novelist Ellen Glasgow didn't kill herself, but left very specific instructions for her burial. She was buried with her French poodle Billy and a Sealyham named Jeremy. (Don't worry, they had already died before her.) She also insisted that she not be buried near her father, whom she hated.

Closing Lines

Henry David Thoreau was asked on his deathbed whether he had made his peace with God. He replied, "I did not know we had ever quarreled."

Said ever-practical Heinrich Heine, "God will pardon me; it's his profession."

Oliver Goldsmith was asked if his conscience was clear. His last words were, "No, it's not."

Oscar Wilde definitely did not say, "Either these curtains or I have got to go." It's slightly possible that he might have observed, "I am dying as I have lived, beyond my means."

Dying of cancer, Gertrude Stein's last words were addressed to her longtime partner, Alice B. Toklas. "What is the answer?" she asked. Toklas couldn't respond. "In that case," Stein quipped weakly, "what's the question?"

H. G. Wells suffered for several minutes with his relatives badgering him for some pithy last words. Finally he rasped impatiently, "Can't you see I'm busy dying?" And then he went and said no more.

As he died, John Greenleaf Whittier gasped out, one word per labored breath, "My—love—to—the—world."

Other writerly last words:

"**T**here will be no proof that I ever was a writer."

> —*Franz Kafka*

"**I**'ve had eighteen straight whiskeys. I think this is a record."

> —*Dylan Thomas*

"**T**ake me away! Take me away!"

> —*Joaquin Miller*

" 'I am about to—or I am going to—die.'
Either expression is used."

> —*Writer and grammarian Dominique Bouhours*

"Now I shall go to sleep."

> —*Lord Byron*

"Let us go in; the fog is rising."

> —*Emily Dickinson*

"So this is Death—well—"

> —*Thomas Carlyle*

"Sister, you're trying to keep me alive as an old curiosity, but I'm done, I'm finished, I'm going to die."

> —*George Bernard Shaw*

"Well, I must arrange my pillows for another weary night. When will this all end?"

> —*Washington Irving*

"**B**efore you quote me, be sure I'm conscious."

—André Gide

"**M**oose . . . Indian."

—Henry David Thoreau

Epitaphs

It's not surprising that writers want to get in the last word. Here are some epitaphs written by writers themselves, not all of which were actually used in the end:

"**H**ere lies one whose name was writ on water."

—John Keats

"**I** had a lover's quarrel with the world."

—Robert Frost

"Good friend for Jesus sake forbeare,
To digg the dust encloased heare:
Bles'e be ye man yt spares thes stones,
And curst be he yt moves my bones."

—*William Shakespeare*

"There is something to be said for being dead."

—*Eugene O'Neill*

"If after I depart this vale you ever remember me and have thought to please my ghost, forgive some sinner and wink your eye at some homely girl."

—*H. L. Mencken*

"The body of
Benjamin Franklin, printer,
(Like the cover of an old book,
Its contents stripped out,
And stript of its lettering and gilding)
Lies here, food for worms!
Yet the work itself shall not be lost,

For it will, as he believed, appear once
more,
In a new
And more beautiful edition,
Corrected and amended
By its Author!"

—*Benjamin Franklin*

"**H**ere lies the body of Jonathan Swift . . .
where, at last savage indignation can no
longer lacerate his heart."

—*Jonathan Swift*

"**P**ardon my dust" and
"If you can read this, you've come too
close."

—*Dorothy Parker*

"**W**hen I am dead, I hope it may be said,
'His sins were scarlet, but his books were
read.'"

—*Hilaire Belloc*

Selected References

Books and Software

The Book of Answers: The New York Public Library Telephone Reference Service's Most Unusual and Entertaining Questions, by Barbara Berliner with Melinda Corey and George Ochoa. Simon and Schuster, 1992.

The Compact Edition of the Oxford English Dictionary. Oxford University Press, 1985.

The Completely Amazing, Slightly Outrageous State Quarters Atlas and Album, by the editors of Klutz. Klutz, Inc., 2001.

Encyclopaedia Britannica, ed. the faculties of the University of Chicago. Benton Publishing, 1979.

The Guinness Book of Records: 1999, by Mark C. Young. Bantam Books, 1999.

Isaac Asimov's Book of Facts: 3,000 of the Most Interesting, Entertaining, Fascinating, Unbelieveable, Unusual and Fantastic Facts, ed. Isaac Asimov. Random House Value Publishing, Inc., 1991.

The Juicy Parts: Things Your History Teacher Never Told You About the 20th Century's Most Famous People, by Jack Mingo. Perigee Books, 1996.

Jumbo Quiz Book. Random House Value Publishing, 1999.

Just Curious About History, Jeeves, by Erin Barrett and Jack Mingo. PocketBooks, 2002.

Just Curious, Jeeves: What Are the 1001 Most Intriguing Questions Asked on the Internet, by Jack Mingo and Erin Barrett. Ask Jeeves, Inc., 2000.

The Ladies' Room Reader: The Ultimate Women's Trivia Book, by Alicia Alvarez. Conari Press, 2001.

The Literary Life and Other Curiosities, by Robert Hendrickson. The Viking Press, 1981.

Microsoft Encarta 98 Encyclopedia, Microsoft 1997.

News from the Fringe: True Stories of Weird People and Weirder Times, compiled by John J. Kohut and Roland Sweet. Plume Books, 1993.

Out of the Mouths of Babes: Quips and Quotes from Wildly Witty Women, by Autumn Stephens. Conari Press, 2001.

The Oxford Dictionary of Quotations, 3rd Edition, by Book Club Associates. Oxford University Press, 1980.

Peter's Quotations: Ideas for Our Time from Socrates to Yogi Berra: Gems of Brevity, Wisdom, and Outrageous Wit, by Dr. Laurence J. Peter. William Morrow and Company, Inc., 1977.

Rotten Rejections, by Andre Bernard. Pushcart Press, 1990.

They Went That-a-Way: How the Famous, the Infamous, and the Great Died, by Malcolm Forbes with Jeff Bloch. Simon and Schuster, 1988.

The 2,548 Best Things Anybody Ever Said, by Robert Byrne. Galahad Books, 1996.

2201 Fascinating Facts, by David Louis. Crown Publishers, Inc., 1988.

An Underground Education: The Unauthorized and Outrageous Supplement to Everything You Thought You Knew About Art, Sex, Business, Crime, Science, Medicine, and Other Fields of Human Knowledge, by Richard Zacks. Anchor Books, 1997.

W. C. Privy's Original Bathroom Companion, ed. Erin Barrett and Jack Mingo. St. Martin's Press, 2003.

Webster's New World Dictionary, 3rd College Edition. Simon & Schuster, Inc., 1988.

Webster's Unabridged Dictionary, 2nd Edition. William Collins & World Publishing Co., Inc. 1976.

Weird History 101, by John Richard Stephens. Adams Media Corporation, 1997.

World Book Encyclopedia. World Book, Inc., 1998.

Online Resources

Electric Library, http://www.elibrary.com/.

Lex Antica, http://members.aol.com/pilgrimjon/private/LEX/LEX.html.

U.S. Department of Labor/Bureau of Labor and Statistics, Occupational Outlook Handbook, http://stats.bls.gov/oco/home.htm.

Useless Information, http://home.nycap.rr.com/useless/contents.html.

The Wholepop Magazine Online, http://www.wholepop.com/.

Acknowledgments

The authors wish to give special thanks to the folks at Conari Press and Red Wheel/Weiser, particularly Leslie Berriman, Brenda Knight, Leah Russell, Pam Suwinsky, Jill Rogers, Liz Wood, and Jan Johnson. They would also like to extend a big thank you to their children, families, and friends for supporting them in pursuing the Writer's Life. Thanks!